The Kids' Guide to Nature Adventures

80 Great Activities for Exploring the Outdoors

The Kids' Guide to Nature Adventures

80 Great Activities for Exploring the Outdoors

Joe Rhatigan

LARK BOOKS

A Division of Sterling Publishing Co., Inc.
New York, NY

Art Director
Stacey Budge

Photographer
Evan Bracken

Cover Photography
John Widman

Cover Designer
Barbara Zaretsky

Illustrator
Olivier Rollin

Production Assistance
Shannon Yokeley
Lorelei Buckley

Assistant Editor
Rain Newcomb

Editorial Assistance
Delores Gosnell

Activity Collaborators
Rain Newcomb
Hope Buttitta

Project Designers
Diana Light
Leslie Huntley

10 9 8 7 6 5 4 3 2 1

First Edition

Published by Lark Books, a division of
Sterling Publishing Co., Inc.
387 Park Avenue South, New York, N.Y. 10016

© 2003, Lark Books

Distributed in Canada by Sterling Publishing,
c/o Canadian Manda Group, One Atlantic Ave., Suite 105
Toronto, Ontario, Canada M6K 3E7

Distributed in the U.K. by Guild of Master Craftsman Publications Ltd., Castle
Place, 166 High Street, Lewes, East Sussex, England
BN7 1XU
Tel: (+ 44) 1273 477374, Fax: (+ 44) 1273 478606, Email: pubs@thegmcgroup.com,
Web: www.gmcpublications.com

Distributed in Australia by Capricorn Link (Australia) Pty Ltd.,
P.O. Box 704, Windsor, NSW 2756 Australia

If you have questions or comments about this book, please contact:
Lark Books
67 Broadway
Asheville, NC 28801
(828) 253-0467

Printed in China

1-57990-373-8

acknowledgements

The following folks were
essential ingredients for this book:
Leslie Huntley, Hope Buttitta, Diana
Light, Leslie Huntley, Joy Harmon at Math
'N' Art, Andy Rae and Lee Speed, Tom Mitchell at
Lake Powatan, Ashlea Allen of the North Carolina Arboretum,
Karen Boekschoten, Rain Newcomb, Terry Krautwurst,
Kathy Holmes, Marcianne Miller, and Sebastian ("Woof.").

Thank you models!
Grace Harrison, Brenda Hill, Leslie Huntley, Terry Lonergan, Ray
Peterson, Corrina Matthews, Cody D. Griffin, Zy Rae, Kia Baden,
Mitch Lind, Connor Lind, Phillip Treadway, Lena Treadway, Forrest
Devitt, Autumn Devitt, Noah Ratner, Nathaniel Humphreys, Gus
Rowan, Dimitri Palmer, Nick Hill, Jake Hill, Mimi Hill, Courtney
Kubitschek, Leah Downey, Karla Weis, Amalia Rowan,
and Jasmine Sky Figlow

Contents

introduction

We look up into the night sky and ask "Where?"

We notice a chrysalis attached to a leaf and ask "When?"

We hear an echo of a wolf's howl and ask "Why?"

We watch a bee at work on a flower and ask "What?"

We sit on a beach watching the tide go out and ask "How?"

We stumble upon a set of strange animal prints in the dried mud and ask "Who?"

Throughout this book, you will find tons of nature activities, projects, ideas, and tidbits that will help you answer these questions (and more!)—and have a lot of fun doing it—whether you're in the backyard, visiting a national park or a beach with your family, camping and hiking in the wilderness, or simply taking a walk in your neighborhood.

Finding nature is easy; it's everywhere. It grows in the cracks in the cement sidewalk. It buzzes in your ear at a cookout. It sings on hot summer nights above the din of the air conditioning. And, if you listen very closely, nature calls to you. It's not something you hear with your ears; your body feels it as a yearning curiosity to touch, see, hear, touch, taste (EXPERIENCE!) what nature has to offer.

Whether you're an experienced outdoors explorer or simply someone who's interested in nature but doesn't know the difference between poison ivy and a petunia, this book has something for you. Read it at home, or take it with you

on your adventures. It's almost impossible to explore nature and not turn into a lifelong student of our fascinating world.

WHAT'S IN IT?
Chapter 1: Take a Hike

One great way to explore nature is to walk in it, whether it's a normal walk or an all-out, all-day hiking adventure. This chapter gives you lots of different ways to experience nature while hiking. There are games to play, things to make, and tips that will make each hike a memorable one.

Chapter 2: Camp Out!

Camping can be a lot of fun, and it doesn't matter if you're camping out in your backyard, at a national park, or in a small clearing where the only noises you hear are the creatures around you. This chapter gets you geared up and ready for one of the greatest nature adventures imaginable.

Chapter 3: Wild Life

Get up close and personal with the animals you may come across while out exploring.

Chapter 4: Mini-Wild Life

Get down on your hands and knees, and explore the mini-creatures of the world who account for up to three-quarters of all the animals on earth.

Chapter 5: Plant Life

Without them, there'd be no life at all. They're easy to get close to (they don't run away), and plants have a whole lot of life in them to explore.

Chapter 6: Explore the Shore

Get your feet wet, and check out life around and in ponds, creeks, lakes, streams, and oceans.

And, finally, **Chapter 7** keeps you up past your bedtime to marvel at the world that wakes up when you're supposed to be asleep.

Native Americans believed every part of the natural world held a gift for humankind. Here's your chance to go out into the world and find it.

CHAPTER ONE

take a hike

If you can only remember one thing about hiking, let it be this: Hiking is not about the "getting there." It's the hike itself, the journey, that provides the adventure. Take your time to explore your surroundings. Stop often, and if you get tired, turn around and head back. A well-planned hike should provide plenty of time for exploring, being with friends and family, snacking, and just being there. This chapter will get you off on the right foot with information on different hikes you can take, things to do while hiking, how to prepare for a hike, and what to bring and make.

the amble

If you've never tried hiking before, start small with a short walk with an adult. You can walk a forest trail, the shoreline of a lake or ocean, or even a short mountain trail.

Take along a fanny pack or a small backpack, and bring these few essentials:

- ✔ An adult
- ✔ A friend (optional)
- ✔ First-aid kit (see page 35)
- ✔ Water bottle
- ✔ Snacks
- ✔ Map of the trail
- ✔ Hat with a wide brim
- ✔ Binoculars (optional)

HELPFUL HINTS

🌿 Never hike by yourself, and stay on the trail.

🌿 With a short hike like this, choose a well-defined hiking trail that is rated "easy."

🌿 Wear comfortable shoes with relatively good traction.

🌿 Find a short, circular trail that ends up where you started.

🌿 Don't carry too much stuff with you.

🌿 There's no rush and no finish line. Take frequent breaks, not only to give yourself a break, but also so you can enjoy your surroundings.

🌿 Don't feel you have to walk the whole trail. If you're getting tired, tell your fellow hikers, and start heading back.

🌿 Leave your surroundings as you found them.

🌿 Dress for the weather.

the day hike

After meandering through a few easy hikes, you may find yourself itching for something more challenging. It's time for the Day Hike, which is exactly what it sounds like: a hike that lasts most of the day. You'll need to pack more stuff, be more careful about what you wear, and be a bit more knowledgeable about where you'll be hiking.

WHAT TO WEAR

Dress for the weather. It's always better to wear several light layers—it's easier to take off extra clothes than to have too few.

Cover your head with a wide-brimmed hat.

A cotton long-sleeved T-shirt, jeans, nylon-blend socks, and comfortable shoes are good for hikes.

Bring a lightweight waterproof jacket.

It's better to be on the cool side than too hot.

Wearing a bandana will keep sweat off your neck.

A lightweight, internal-frame backpack with a hip belt will make your load feel lighter and more managable.

WHAT TO PACK

Be smart about what you think you "must have" with you. In other words, leave the science textbook and CD player home.

Essentials
These are the must-have items:
✔ A comfortable backpack

✔ Detailed trail map

✔ At least 1 liter of water in a canteen, thermos, or wide-mouthed bottle

✔ Whistle, in case you get lost

✔ Identification and emergency money

✔ Watch

✔ Food for the hike, as well as snacks, and two emergency high-protein energy bars

✔ Toilet paper and a trowel

✔ Compass

✔ First-aid kit

✔ Flashlight

✔ Pocket knife (make sure it's okay with your parents)

✔ Extra socks, especially if you know you'll be crossing streams

✔ Bug spray

✔ Orange garbage bag, for an emergency poncho

✔ Garbage bag

✔ Matches or other source of fire (let adults carry)

Optional Items
✔ Field guide

✔ Mobile phone, if you have one

✔ Hiking stick (see page 19)

✔ Rope

✔ Camera

✔ Binoculars

✔ Water purifying tablets

✔ Notebook and pencil to jot down notes

HELPFUL HINTS

Once again, never hike alone. Hiking is a group sport, and you should always have an adult with you, especially on these longer hikes where the possibility of getting lost is greater.

Stick to the trails. Creating your own path might get you lost, and you'll damage plant life.

Get home before dark. Depending on where you're hiking, you'll probably average about 2 miles an hour. Count how many hours of daylight you have, and leave enough time to get back.

Keep yourself hydrated: Drink water before you feel thirsty.

Plan your outings and create a shopping list of what you'll need to bring.

Pack your food in tightly sealed containers.

Don't overfill your pack. Take turns wearing the heaviest pack, or distribute your gear evenly.

Know what to expect. Talk to a park ranger if you're hiking at a National Park, or talk to someone who has hiked the trail before. You also can find information online. Will you be walking through water? Bring extra socks. Climbing rocks? Make sure your boots or shoes have good traction. Up hill? Consider a hiking stick.

Be aware of the ever-changing weather (see page 20).

Always bring your own water, and don't drink the water in creeks unless you have a way to purify it.

happy feet

If your feet are not happy, your hike will be miserable. That doesn't mean you have to go out and buy the most expensive hiking boots in the world. A good pair of tennis shoes is usually more than enough support for many hikes. In fact, tennis shoes that fit well and have good traction are better than poorly made boots that fall apart and don't fit. But here are some tips for keeping you and your feet hiking.

Make sure your shoes or hiking boots are comfortable. That means your feet don't slide around in them; your toes aren't crunched up, etc.

If possible, wear shoes or boots that support your ankles. Avoid sandals.

Don't wear new shoes on the trail. Break them in by wearing them to school for a week or by going on some walks around your neighborhood.

For longer hikes, don't wear all-cotton socks. They absorb too much sweat and moisture. Wear wool- and nylon-blend socks. They breathe moisture out, rather than soak it up. Also, make sure your socks fit properly and don't bunch down into your shoes.

Make sure your shoes have good traction.

Umm. . .time for a new pair of shoes.

BEATING BLISTERS

Even if you follow all the advice in the world, you may still find yourself with a blister, the dreaded bane of all hikers' existence. What to do?

✚ If you feel a blister coming on (it will feel like a hot spot), stop walking. Take off your shoe, readjust your sock, and look for possible causes. Protect the skin with a bandage, moleskin, or, if those are too thick, a piece of duct tape (it really works).

✚ If a blister does form, don't break it! First of all, it's gross. Second, and more importantly, the fluid inside the blister actually protects the skin. Instead, create a "doughnut" bandage by cutting out a hole the size of the blister in the middle of the bandage. Then place it so the blister ends up in the hole where it can breathe. This reduces friction and protects the skin.

leave only footprints

Back in the old days, discovering nature usually meant finding, killing, and bringing home animals, bugs, and plant life. Over the years, naturalists figured out that watching all sorts of life in their natural surroundings was a much better way. Plus, with today's concern for habitat and endangered species, it's simply inhumane and selfish to take nature home with you. These objects are all valuable pieces that serve purposes right where they are. Here are some guidelines to follow when on the trail or anywhere you come across nature:

📷 Take pictures or sketches, and take everything out that you brought in with you.

📷 Know the rules and guidelines of where you're hiking. Most parks, arboretums, and campgrounds prohibit anyone from taking flowers, insects, and small reptiles.
If you're not sure, don't.

📷 If you're allowed to collect flower specimens or rocks, take only what you absolutely need. Make sure you leave plenty behind. Never pick rare plants, and don't uproot anything.

📷 Be gentle with any creature you catch (including insects!), and set it free when you've finished checking them out.

what's your pace?

Your pace is not only how fast you can walk, but also how far you travel with each step. This is good information to have on the trail if you want to figure out how far you're walking.

WHAT YOU NEED
Tape measure
2 sticks
Paper and pencil

WHAT YOU DO

1 Measure out 100 feet of flat ground, and mark it with the sticks.

2 Walk the 100 feet at a normal pace. Count how many times your right foot comes down. Write down the number. Do this four more times, each time writing down the number.

3 Add the five numbers and divide by five. That will give you your average pace for 100 feet.

4 For your pace length, divide 100 feet by the average of your five measurements. For example, if your right foot came down 20 times on average, divide 100 by 20, which is 5 feet per pace.

5 If you want to know how many steps you'll take on a particular hike, multiply the trail's length by 5,280 (the number of feet in a mile) to get the hike's length in feet. For example, if you're planning to hike a 4-mile trail, multiply 4 x 5,280, which equals 21,120. Divide this number by your average pace length. For example, 21,120 divided by 5 (your average pace length) equals 4,224. Multiply this by 2 (each pace is two steps) for the average number of steps you'll take on that hike. Pretty impressive, eh?!

hiking stick

A good hiking stick will come in handy when the trail is steep or rocky. It will steady you when you cross a creek, and, most of all, it will give you something to lean on when you're at the end of a long hike.

WHAT YOU NEED

Sturdy stick, about shoulder height

Sharp pocket knife (first, get an adult's permission)

Soft leather strip (optional)

Acrylic paints

Paintbrush

Bells (optional)

Twine (optional)

WHAT YOU DO

1 Find just the right stick. Walk around with it a bit to get a feel for it. Make sure it's not too short, and find out where your hand is most comfortable on it when walking.

2 If you want, peel off the bark with the knife, or carve designs into the wood. You can also carve sections of bark off and paint designs on the bare wood.

3 If you want, wrap the grip area with a soft leather strip to cushion your hand. If you're leaving the bark on the stick, you can carve off the bark where you'll hold it.

4 When hiking in bear country, tie several loud bells to the twine. Tie the twine around the top of the stick. This gives any bears the chance to run off when they hear you jingling. They're just as unhappy to see you as you are to see them.

5 Another cool trick for decorating your stick is to cut a design on the bark of the stick, and place the stick in a campfire until the carved portion of the stick is charred. Remove the stick, let it cool, and then strip off the rest of the bark. You'll have a cool, wood-burned design.

read the weather

Even if the forecast calls for clear skies all day, there's always the chance that the weather could change during your hike. You can rely on your own senses and knowledge to tell you of approaching bad weather.

Fair weather is ahead if:

- You see wispy thin clouds up above
- Dandelion flowers are open
- Geese and crows are flying high in the sky
- The sunrise or sunset is yellow and mellow
- The wind is gentle and blowing from the west or northwest
- Pinecones are open

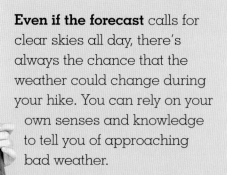

Foul weather may be ahead if:

 You feel a sudden drop in temperature and change in direction and strength of the wind. A thunderstorm may be on its way.

 Dandelion flowers and pinecones are closed

 Birds are flying low in the sky and are lining up on wires

There's a ring around the sun or moon. These light rings are caused by light refracted through ice crystals high in the atmosphere. There will be rain usually within a day or two.

 Flies are biting

There's a red sunrise

There are dark, fast-moving clouds forming in the west

how close is that thunderstorm?

You're in the middle of an awesome hike when suddenly you hear the rumbling of an approaching storm. To figure out how close it is, count the seconds between the flash of lightning and the clap of thunder, and divide by five. That's how many miles away the lightning struck. If it's one or two miles, you're within striking distance. You probably know that it's a bad move to hide under a tree, but what should you do?

Don't be the highest object around. Squat and ball yourself up so you're as low as possible without lying down. Keep your bottom off the ground. Wrap your arms around your legs, close your eyes, and keep your feet together. Make sure you're not touching anything metallic.

Make sure your hiking group separates at least 50 feet from each other to minimize multiple injuries.

A forest of even-height trees is relatively safe.

Stay out of caves and avoid cliff bases.

When hiking, frequently look up at the sky, and if you see dark clouds and hear thunder, turn back immediately.

poison ivy, bees, mosquitos, oh, my!

Along with all the good stuff that nature has to offer comes the itchy stuff. Poisonous plants, stinging bugs, and blood-sucking creatures can drive a hiker nuts. The only solution is to know these things exist, know where you're hiking, and what potential hazards may be around, and hope for the best.

POISONOUS PLANTS

If you brush past poison ivy, you may not even know about it until a day or two later. By then it's too late. Here comes the itching. If you realize you've come into contact with poison ivy, or its close cousin poison oak, take a cool bath as soon as possible, and thoroughly soap yourself clean. If you can't take a bath, clean your skin with rubbing alcohol. Use calamine

Poison ivy has three pointed, shiny, dark green leaves with jagged edges and slightly hairy undersides along with gray-white berries.

lotion or other poison ivy medication. See a doctor if you develop a fever and have flu-like symptoms. Also, wash your clothes, touching them as little as possible.

BEE STING RELIEF

Sooner or later, you may find yourself with a throbbing, swelling bee sting.Unless you're allergic, this mishap is only fatal to the bee, who not only loses his stinger, but his lower abdomen as well (ouch).

After removing the stinger, wash your wound before applying any of these pain and swelling remedies to your wound: toothpaste, baking soda and water, ear wax, meat tenderizer mixed with a little bit of water, a bag of frozen food or ice cubes, or a cloth soaked in cold water, mud, onion slices, vinegar and clay, or a piece of lean raw meat.

If you're allergic to bees, make sure you have your proper medication with you before your hike.

MOSQUITOES

To minimize mosquito madness, wear light-colored clothing that covers as much skin as possible, use bug repellent, and when bitten, try rubbing the bite with lemon juice or garlic cloves.

should you worry about bears?

Even though bears are not the cute, cuddly toy-like creatures portrayed in kids' books, they're also not ferocious man-eaters. If given the chance, most bears avoid people.

Your best defense is to stay alert and look for bear signs, such as claw marks on trees, tracks, droppings, trampled vegetation, or over-turned and broken, rotten logs. Talking loudly, wearing bells, and even singing are all good ways to warn bears you're nearby.

Talk to local naturalists, park rangers, or other hikers to determine if you should be prepared for possible bear sightings, and what is the best way to deal with a bear encounter.

follow the leader

Use the natural "symbols" below to create directional markers for your hiking buddies to follow. Leave a snack at the end of the trail as an incentive.

WHAT YOU NEED
A familiar trail
Several friends
At least two adults
Two trail maps
Rocks, twigs, grass, etc.
Plenty of snacks

WHAT YOU DO

1 Split the hiking group into two groups, with at least one adult in each group.

2 Decide which group will go first and set the trail. Set boundaries such as "no turning off trail paths."

3 The first group should first gather around their map, and decide where their ending point will be, and how they'll get there. Once that's established, they can set off.

4 At the first intersection in the path, build a signal for the second group to follow so they know which way to go. Keep leaving signals until you're at your destination. They should then wait for the second group with the snacks.

5 After snacks, let the second group go first. Keep playing until the hike's over.

Go straight

Turn right

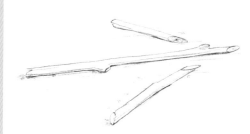

Go straight

Turn right

Turn left

Turn left

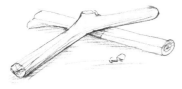

Not this way

take a .

something, hike for a half mile, and sit down again. Don't get up until you spot some more wildlife.

MINI-HIKE

Get on your hands and knees, and instead of taking a 100-mile hike, take a 100-inch hike. Bring along a magnifying glass, and start crawling.

RAIN HIKE

Put on your rain gear and take a walk in the rain (as long as there's no threat of lightning!). You'll find that the world is a different place. It sounds different. It smells different. And once you get used to being wet, you'll have fun.

BLIND HIKE

Working in pairs, have one hiker blindfold the other, and lead her on a "blind" hike. Make sure the blindfolded hiker has a chance to smell and touch things. Then, switch places.

SILENT HIKE

No talking, please.

compass hunt

This game is actually a sneaky way to get you used to using a compass.

WHAT YOU NEED
Stick
Compass
Paper and pencil
A friend

WHAT YOU DO

1 Mark your starting point with a stick or "X" marked on the ground.

2 Choose your first landmark (for example, a nearby picnic table).

direction of travel line

the case

bearing

3 Hold your compass at chest level so that the direction-of-travel line points to your landmark.

4 Turn the case until the north end of the compass needle (often red) is pointing at the N symbol.

5 Read the bearing (for example, 300°) where the direction-of-travel line intersects the case's dial.

6 Now, holding your compass still and keeping the bearing the same, begin walking toward your landmark. Count the number of paces to your landmark from your starting point. Record your bearing and paces on a piece of paper. This will be your first clue.

7 Once you reach your first landmark, look around for a second one. Take a bearing to it, and pace it off. This will be your second clue. Continue this process until you have at least six clues. Now give the clues to your friend and see if he can find his way.

staying found

Even when taking every precaution, hikers still get lost sometimes. Here are some ways to stay found:

⚐ Let someone back home know where you and your fellow hikers will be going and approximately when you'll be back. Leave an extra map at home.

⚐ Pay attention to landmarks, and turn around and look behind you, so you'll know what to look for on the way back.

LOST?

If you do get lost, the first thing to do is to stop walking. Stay in one place. If you keep wandering, you'll waste energy, and end up being harder to find.

Also:

⚐ Stay with your hiking buddies, and stay close together to stay warm.

⚐ Stay dry, and find a cozy waiting place, such as under a tree.

⚐ Blow your whistle, and call for help. Blow three times, pause, blow three more times, and so on.

⚐ Don't sit on the bare ground. Create a mattress of leaves.

⚐ Put out something bright, such as white paper, and make signals (see page 24).

⚐ Don't eat anything you're not sure of: no berries or mushrooms.

⚐ Stay away from large rivers and lakes, and only drink dew off leaves.

nature snapshot

During one of your hiking breaks, create a "human camera," and play this eye-opening game of nature clues.

WHAT YOU NEED
A partner

WHAT YOU DO

1 Decide who will be the "camera," and who will be the "photographer."

2 The camera should close his eyes and keep them closed. It might be helpful for the photographer to put his hands over the camera's eyes.

3 The photographer should carefully guide the camera (remember, he can't see!) to a particular spot in the wilderness where the first clue is found. Watch for large rocks and sticks where the camera could stumble.

4 The photographer then removes his hands for about two seconds, then quickly replaces them. This is his first "picture." The photographer then continues to guide the camera to other clues. Five to seven clues should be enough.

5 Return to your starting point. The camera should now guess what all the "pictures" had in common.

IDEAS FOR THEMES:

▷ places where animals live

▷ signs of humans

▷ things that are gross

▷ things animals eat

▷ hiding places for animals

▷ things that are green (or red, yellow, etc.)

▷ things that are circles or squares

In all things of nature there is something of the marvelous.

–Aristotle

hiking snacks

So what can you take to eat on your hike? Sandwiches are good, as long as you put them in plastic containers that will protect them from getting squashed. Dried or fresh fruits, nuts, vegetables, and even some cookies will also do the trick. Store-bought trail mixes are good, but not as good as one you can make yourself.

THE-WHATEVER-YOU-FIND-IN-THE-KITCHEN-CABINET MIX

Get a large bowl and fill it with nuts, dry cereal, seeds, dried fruits, raisins, chocolate chips, pretzels, sesame sticks, bite-size bagel chips, and anything else you think might taste good thrown in. In order to get just the right taste, put a little bit of your found items in at a time until you have just the right flavor. Place the mixture in self-sealing plastic bags. If you really feel adventurous, sprinkle some spices into the mix, but don't overdo it.

GORP (GOOD OL' RAISINS AND PEANUTS)

The name says it all, though, of course, you make this one to suit your own tastes. For best results, make sure you have a good mix of crunchy, salty foods, and sweet, chewy items.

camp out!

Camping is just about everyone's idea of what it means to get in touch with nature and get away from it all. A camping adventure (whether it's in the backyard, a campsite, or some remote area of the wilderness) doesn't have to be an expensive proposition. You can make a lot of the gear you'll need simply and cheaply. Read on for great tips, easy projects, and great camping fun.

homemade backpack

This is a fun backpack you can make that's perfect for a short hike or trek to your campsite.

WHAT YOU NEED
Old jeans
2 pieces of rope, about
  1-foot long
  each
Belt

WHAT YOU DO

1 Lay the jeans facedown on a table. Bring the leg bottoms up to the back belt loops.

2 Scrunch up one leg hole, and tie it with one of the pieces of rope, closing up the leg opening. Leave enough rope on either side of the knot, and tie the leg to a back belt loop. Repeat with the other leg.

3 Thread the belt through the belt loops of the jeans.

4 Fill up your backpack with your stuff, and use the belt to close up the waist of the jeans. Decorate as needed!

BUYING A BACKPACK?

If you're going on an extended camping trip that calls for carrying a lot of gear for long amounts of time, buy a backpack with a hipbelt. The hipbelt will transfer a lot of the weight of the pack to your hips, and you'll be able to carry more stuff comfortably. Also consider buying a pack with an internal frame.

instant tent

A tent is your temporary house while you camp. It will keep you dry and warm (or cool), and protect you from whatever nature decides to throw at you. These three tents are perfect for mild-weather camping where there aren't too many bugs.

WHAT YOU NEED

10 x 12-foot (can be slightly smaller) tarp with grommets (holes along edges)

Smaller tarp (to sleep on)

50 feet or more of braided nylon rope

Several tent stakes

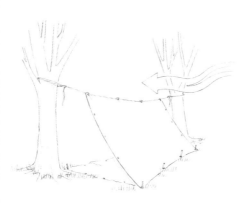

ROOF TENT

1 Find two trees that are about 10 to 12 feet apart. Decide which way the wind is blowing, and make sure you put up the tarp so it blocks it.

2 Thread the nylon rope through the grommet holes in the end of the tarp that will be attached to the trees.

3 Tie the two corners to the trees about 6 (or more) feet off the ground. Use a good sturdy knot that won't slip, such as the clove hitch on page 36. If you can't climb the tree, have an adult help you.

4 Stake the other side of the tarp to the ground.

EASY A-FRAME

1 Find two trees 10 feet apart. Tie each end of the rope to the trees about 6 to 8 feet off the ground, using a good sturdy knot such as the clove hitch. Make sure the rope is taut.

2 Throw the tarp over rope, and stake the corners.

camping utility belt

Great for hiking and wearing around the campsite, this belt can be altered for whatever purpose you need it for: mobile first-aid kit, snack center, collections holder, whatever.

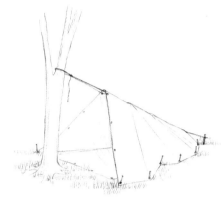

ONE-TREE TENT

1 Tie one end of the rope to a tree about 7 to 10 feet high. Throw the tarp over the rope.

2 Tie the other end of the rope to a very large tent peg or strong stick. Pull the rope away from the tree until you have the tarp in the desired position. Pound the stake or stick into the ground.

3 Pull the tarp taut and stake it to the ground. If the tent is slipping, tie some rope from the top of the tent, and tie this rope to the tree.

WHAT YOU NEED

Thick army belt with little
  grommet holes*
Elastic
Scissors
Heavy-duty, self-adhesive,
  hook-and-loop tape or
  epoxy glue
Film canisters
Assorted hooks, clips,
  key rings, etc.

* These can be found at army surplus stores. You can also use a normal belt if you can punch holes in it with an awl or a pair of scissors.

WHAT YOU DO

1 Decide what purpose your belt will serve. Make sure it fits comfortably.

2 Cut a piece of elastic, and attach it to the belt with the hook-and-loop tape, leaving space for the film canisters so they fit between the belt and the elastic.

3 Attach your hooks, clips, and key rings, and add your supplies to your belt. Make sure nothing bangs against your legs—that will annoy you.

make your own sleeping bag

Half the fun of camping is collecting the gear you'll need. Sure, you could go ahead and buy most of your stuff—and if you get serious about camping, you should—but if you're just starting out on the adventure of camping, think about making your own stuff, whether it's for a real camping trip or simply a practice-run in the backyard.

WHAT YOU NEED

Plastic rain poncho
   or tarpaulin (tarp)
2 blankets
Sheet

WHAT YOU DO

1 Place the poncho on the ground. Put the first blanket on top of the poncho.

2 Lay the second blanket down on top of the first blanket. Make sure the second blanket is not bigger than the first one. If it is, move it up so the bottom of the first blanket shows.

3 Fold the top blanket in thirds, and pin it together to form sort of a burrito shape.

4 Fold and pin the bottom of the first blanket over the second blanket burrito. Pin the first blanket's edges together.

5 Position the pinned blankets so they line up with the poncho or tarp. Fold the tarp over the blankets, and if possible, snap the poncho shut. Then, roll up your sleeping bag, and use rope or belts to keep it rolled up until you're ready to use it.

first-aid kit

SLEEPING BAG ESSENTIALS

🌲 Don't forget to bring a headrest or pillow and a sleeping pad.

🌲 For an instant pillow, inflate a large self-sealing plastic bag, and seal it shut.

🌲 If you want to buy a sleeping bag, it must be comfortable and the right rating for the weather you'll encounter. For mild to hot conditions, a three-season (spring through fall) bag will be perfect. It will keep you warm even if the temperature drops to 20°F. You can buy sleeping bags for some serious cold winter camping as well.

🌲 You can purchase a down bag, which is light, warm, and compressible, but it must stay dry. Synthetic bags cost less and insulate even when wet.

All good things are wild and free.

—Henry David Thoreau

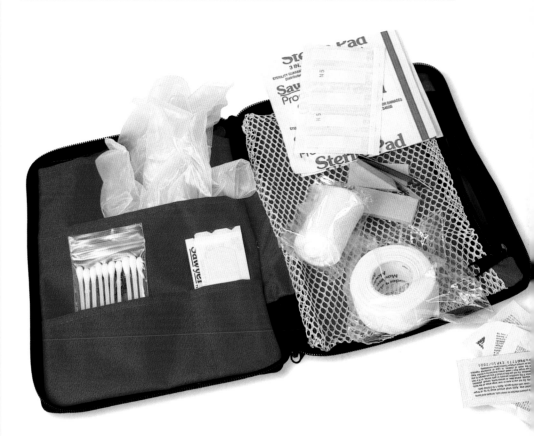

Here's one "thing to bring" that you hope won't be needed, but hey, accidents happen. Here's what to include in a first-aid kit:

✔ Easily identifiable holder
✔ Personal medication
✔ Bandages
✔ Moleskin (for blisters— see page 17)
✔ Medical tape

✔ Sterile gauze pads
✔ Antibiotic wipes
✔ Antiseptic cream
✔ Burn ointment
✔ Sunburn lotion
✔ Hydrogen peroxide
✔ Scissors
✔ Tweezers
✔ Eye wash
✔ Calamine lotion
✔ Thin rubber gloves
✔ First-aid manual

knuts about knots

Impress your friends and family with a few easy knots that will make your camping experience just a little bit easier.

CLOVE HITCH

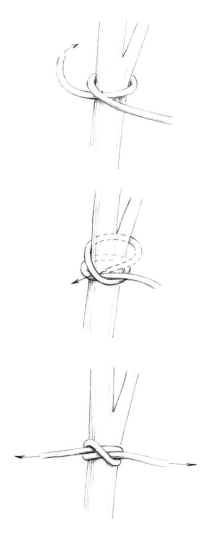

This knot is good for tying a line to a tree.

TAUTLINE HITCH

This one is used for adjusting the tension of tent lines. It can be slipped to tighten or loosen a line. It's perfect for putting up tarp tents.

CONSTRICTOR KNOT

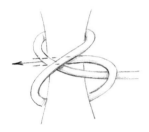

This knot is good for tying up your smellables bag (see page 42).

BOWLINE

This very useful knot creates a secure loop that won't unravel. You can tie it around objects.

duct tape: don't leave home without it

When campers run into problems with their gear, what do you turn to? Their roll of duct tape, of course! What's so good about duct tape, anyway? First of all, it's tough, and waterproof. Second, you can tear it easily with your hands, and it sticks to just about anything. Use it to repair a damaged shoe in the middle of a hike. Fix the broken strap on your backpack. Close up the rip in your tent, the tear in your tarp, the leak in your air mattress. Duct tape is also a great quick-fix for sleeping bags, ponchos, fishing poles, your noisy little brother (only kidding) ... it could even help you out when your knots don't work out.

camping checklist

When camping at a national park or campsite, use this page as a checklist to prepare for the adventure.

CHOOSING THE PERFECT CAMPSITE

🌲 Get to your campsite early in the day, way before the sun sets. You don't want to have to pitch your tent in the dark, and you don't want to wake up in a patch of poison ivy.

🌲 Find a dry, level and shaded area that's relatively high. If you camp at the bottom of a slope, you may find yourself flooded out during a rainstorm.

🌲 Make sure the restroom, bathing, and garbage disposal facilities are within a reasonable distance.

🌲 Make sure there's a drinkable water supply nearby. There's nothing worse than having to hike three miles carrying a five-gallon bucket of water.

🌲 Don't create a new site; use established and acceptable camping locations.

🌲 Look for poison ivy, and remove rocks and branches before pitching the tent.

HOW TO BE A CONSIDERATE CAMPER

🍃 Pick up litter, even if it's not yours.

🍃 Keep the noise level low. Or, if you're going to have a loud singalong, invite your camping neighbors, and stop at a reasonable hour.

🍃 Know what's allowed and what's not at that particular campsite.

WHAT TO BRING

✔ Tent

✔ Sleeping bag

✔ Air or foam sleeping pad

✔ Pillow

✔ Biodegradable soap for you and the dishes

✔ No-rinse soap

✔ Large container for water

✔ Toilet paper in self-sealed plastic bag

✔ Towels

✔ Personal hygiene stuff

✔ First-aid kit (see page 35)

✔ Binoculars

✔ Field guides

✔ Camera

✔ Bug spray

✔ Cards and games

✔ This book

✔ Pen and paper

✔ Compass (if you know how to use one—see page 26)

✔ Duct tape (see page 37)

✔ Flashlight

✔ Lantern

✔ Cooking utensils

✔ Rope

✔ Whistle (see page 27)

✔ Proper clothing for the weather and terrain

✔ Hat

✔ Food (see page 40)

FOOD AND COOKING TIPS

✂ Dried foods are very convenient, though perhaps not always all that tasty.

✂ Bring a cooler and a bunch of tie-down cords to "lock" it.

✂ Your main meals should be cooked on a camp stove, but bring marshmallows if you're going to build a campfire at some point.

✂ Put together a toolbox with all the kitchen utensils you'll need, such as a can opener, spatula, etc.

✂ Measure ingredients for favorite recipes ahead of time, and pack them in self-sealing plastic bags—don't forget to label them.

✂ Precook food items ahead of time (noodles, rice, etc.), freeze them, and put them in the cooler.

✂ Don't forget aluminum foil.

✂ Keep pots covered when cooking. The food will cook quicker, and you won't use as much fuel.

✂ Pita bread, bagels, and English muffins pack better than loaves of bread.

✂ Bring plenty of easy-to-eat snacks: granola bars, dried fruit, beef jerky, trail mix, etc.

campsite detective

You found the *perfect* campsite. Yea! Now, before you set up your stuff, play this simple game to determine who was here before you.

Have everyone you're camping with spread out over the site looking for evidence of previous campers. You may find a fire ring, litter, old smelly socks, footprints, or rope tied to a tree. Bring all the stuff you find to the center of the campsite, and see if you can figure out who camped here. This is also a great way to clean up any mess before setting up camp. Remember, leave the site even better than the way you found it.

pitch a tent blindfolded

Why? Well, imagine you get lost, and don't arrive at your campsite until dark. Will you be able to pitch your tent? After doing this activity, you *might*.

WHAT YOU NEED
Three friends
A tent
Two blindfolds

WHAT YOU DO

1 Choose one person to remain unblindfolded to give instructions when needed, take pictures, and laugh.

2 Blindfold the two tent pitchers. Put the tent equipment in front of them, and let them go at it.

3 The unblindfolded person can give advice, directions, hints, as he sees fit. Or not. His choice. Use this activity as a reminder to get to your campsite early—unless you want to wake all the rest of the campers in the area with your laughter.

where to leave the leftovers

Unfortunately, many animals like the taste of human food. It isn't good for them, and it certainly isn't good to have them foraging around your campsite looking for it. So where do you put your food items? In a "smellables" bag, of course!

WHAT YOU NEED

Tall tree
At least 50 feet of braided nylon rope
Rock or shoe
Empty sleeping bag sack
Your leftovers

WHAT YOU DO

1 When you first get to your campsite, find a tall tree with a branch at least 15 to 20 feet off the ground. The higher the better.

2 Tie a rock or someone's shoe to one of the ends of the rope, and toss that end over the branch. Don't worry; you'll get it sooner or later.

3 Untie the rock or shoe, and pull both ends of the rope to make sure the branch is strong enough. If not, duck.

4 Tie one end to the tree (see "Knuts for Knots" on page 36). Leave the other end hanging until after dinner.

5 After your yummy meal, pack leftovers, candy bars, soap, toothpaste (brush your teeth first), and anything else that's smelly into the empty sleeping bag sack.

6 Tie the free end of the rope to the sack (use a constrictor knot—see page 37). Untie the other end of the rope, and pull the bag up at least 10 to 15 feet, and at least 4 feet below the branch.

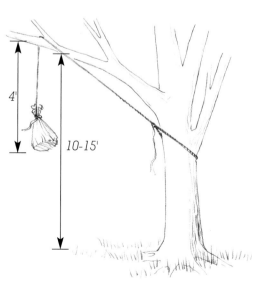

4'

10-15'

OTHER TIPS FOR AVOIDING HUNGRY ANIMALS

 Don't feed any animals you come across.

Store your food in the car if it's nearby.

Never leave food in your tent.

Change out of the clothes you cooked in.

 Remember, even a small animal can do a lot of damage to your tent and campsite.

the scoop on campfires

Build fires only when it's safe to do so. Don't start a fire during dry or windy weather.

Never leave a fire unattended.

Build fires only in locations where you can find plenty of dead wood on the ground.

Build the fire in an existing fire ring.

Gather wood from a wide area away from camp. This keeps the area from becoming depleted.

Leave the site as natural and pleasant-looking as you found it (or better).

Never build a fire underneath tree branches or atop surface roots.

Keep a bucket of water and shovel nearby.

Don't build the fire near tents.

 Don't use flammable fluids to start the fire. Use matches.

Don't forget the marshmallows.

Many campsites and national parks no longer allow campers to start fires. That doesn't mean you can't all convene in a circle to tell stories, sing, and simply enjoy each other's company. Instead of a fire, you can put a lantern on the ground for everyone to gather around. Or, tell everyone to bring a flashlight. How about bringing along a bunch of glowsticks? Use your imagination.

telling campfire ghost stories

The stars are out, and all eyes are on you. Waiting. Fortunately, the audience is on your side; most of us love a good scare. Follow these basic guidelines, and you'll keep your listeners on the edge of their seats and up all night.

🔥 Set the mood ahead of time by dropping little hints about a story you want to tell later.

🔥 If you have a campfire, let the fire die to a low glow, or light a few candles. Use a flashlight as a last resort.

🔥 Change the story, if necessary, to make it as up-to-date as possible. The most effective ghost stories are about regular people and set in the recent past.

🔥 Make the story personal: "My friend has a cousin who was camping once …" or "Just up the road not far from here …." Good ghost stories are usually told as if they're true.

🔥 Pause often while telling the story. Let the sounds of the night around you creep in. Wait for your audience to urge you to go on. Pretend like it's too painful to say any more.

🔥 If you think you can pull it off, stop completely before you reach the story's scary finish to ask if anyone else heard anything ("oh, it was probably nothing"), then search the area with a flashlight to be sure. An out of-sight accomplice can add sound effects such as rustling branches or a good old blood-curdling scream.

🔥 Make your finish more riveting by threatening to withhold the ending (you've decided it's just too scary), or by suggesting that you wait to tell how it turns out another time. Your audience will beg you to finish the tale.

bang-a-pot singalong

Get a bunch of people out in nature after dinner, and what do they want to do? Sing, of course. Here's one way to get everyone involved, even if only a few people know any of the words to the songs.

WHAT YOU NEED

Bug book (see below)
Pots and pans
Sticks
Plastic food containers
Dry beans or pebbles
Spoons
Cool songs to sing
Whatever else you can find

WHAT YOU DO

1 Before the camping trip, have everyone who's going with you find the words to a few of their favorite songs. Make sure they are songs that are fairly easy to sing along to. Folk songs, traditional camping songs, summer camp songs, and even some pop tunes will work. Have your fellow campers write down the words.

2 Make photocopies for everyone, and put them in binders to bring with you on the trip. If someone plays guitar, try to find out the chords for the songs. (Why is it called a "bug book"? Well, sitting around with flashlights, lanterns, or a campfire tends to attract bugs, and in a pinch, these binders make good mosquito swatters!)

3 Find or create something to beat, shake, or bang. Fill an empty food container with dry beans or pebbles. Bang a pot with a wooden spoon. Place two spoons bowl to bowl in one hand between your thumb and middle finger. Shake the spoons loosely in your hands. Strike them against your thigh. With practice it will make a cool, rhythmic sound. Turn over a five-gallon container and beat it with your hands.

4 Once everyone has an instrument, practice getting a rhythm going, open the bug book, and start with a song everyone knows. If that's not working, try "Home on the Range." That should warm everyone up. Have campers sing a few lines of an unfamiliar song until everyone can pick it up.

5 When you're done singing, keep shaking, banging, slapping, and chanting. Experiment, improvise, and stop before it gets too late—your camping neighbors might get annoyed.

2 Have each participant copy the list in their notepad, with one item having a page by itself.

3 Start searching. Don't veer far off any trails without an adult's permission. Once you find something, take a moment to describe it in your notepad, sketch it, write a quick poem about it. Don't just check it off, and don't rush. Make sure you and your friends don't turn this into a crazy competition. This is just a way to look more closely at nature, and then share what you found with your friends.

scavenger hunt

Before setting off to explore with some friends or family, create a list of things to find out in nature. Instead of collecting the items, which isn't so nice for the habitat, simply draw what you've found.

WHAT YOU NEED

Small notepads
Pencils or pens

WHAT YOU DO

1 Come up with a list of things to find on your hike. The list can vary from specific items such as pinecones, rotten logs, and owl pellets, to animal prints, mushrooms, "signs of animal life," and "places where animals may live."

wild

You've probably seen dozens of photographs and illustrations of foxes, but have you ever seen a real fox? Foxes, like most animals, are shy, and quite frankly, that's a good thing. Their survival depends upon avoiding possible enemies. While exploring nature, you may unexpectedly come across a deer, beaver, snake, etc., but more likely, you'll see signs of past animal activity before you see the actual animal. But, with a little patience, you can find where these animals live, what they eat, where they've been, and if you really work at it, you might meet some of them.

camouflage

The best way to observe wildlife is to make sure wildlife doesn't observe you first. Create this blind to hide yourself in nature.

WHAT YOU NEED
Large burlap or white sheet
Scissors
Green and brown paint
Paintbrush
String

Cut three or four rectangular slits in the [clo]th for peepholes. Don't make [the] holes too big, but make sure [the]re's enough clearance for [bin]oculars to fit through.

Pack some snacks and water, and let a parent or [gu]ardian know where you're [go]ing. Choose snacks you can [ch]ew without making a lot of [noi]se. Also, don't forget your [bin]oculars and camera. If you

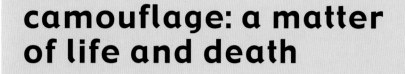

camouflage: a matter of life and death

can, choose a spot where you've seen animals or birds before. Find a good hiding spot where you can place the blind. Try the edge of a field, forest, pond, or creek, or behind some shrubs and tall grass. Tie the blind to tree trunks, shrub branches, or to two wooden stakes in the ground. Make sure that none of the edges will flap in the breeze.

6 Place sticks, fallen branches, and other natural debris to further camouflage the blind.

7 Wait. (Don't give up after 10 minutes.)

Note: If you don't want to build a blind, you can sit in a tent or car and wait. Or, just sit down, and stop moving for an hour or so. Or at least don't make any sudden movements. Soon you'll become just another nonthreatening piece of the landscape.

Imagine you're about to become lunch. What do you do? Run? No way. Your predator is much faster than you. Attack? Bad move. Stop moving, hold your breath, and stay perfectly still? Okay, now you've got a fighting chance, especially if you've got a little camouflage helping you out. Animals, insects, and even plants have perfected blending in with their environment, especially if they don't have other skills such as speed or strength to help them survive. Here are some examples:

A walking stick hanging out in a tree will most likely escape the notice of birds if it remains still.

A hare will remain motionless in a field, blending in with the grass.

Some animals can match their environment's color or pattern, so, if they live in soil, they're soil-colored, or in snow; they're white.

So, if you don't want to become somebody's next meal, keep still, and pray you have camouflage on your side. Oh, by the way, camouflage isn't only used by the not so fast and not so strong. Many predators are also on to the camouflage thing. Watch out!

using binoculars

A good pair of binoculars can really bring wildlife up close. You may be able to see subtle features and behavior patterns you wouldn't be able to see with just your eyes. And you don't have to buy a super-expensive model to enjoy a much improved view.

BINOCULAR TIPS:

When shopping for binoculars, make sure you test them out in the store first.

Binoculars are described using a two-number code such as "7 x 36" or "8 x 42."

The first number usually ranges from 7 to 10 and refers to the binocular's magnification power. So, if an object is viewed through a 10x binocular, it will appear 10 times larger than if seen with only the naked eye.

The second number refers to the size in millimeters of the front lens. Most binoculars range from 20 to 60 millimeters. This number determines how much light is captured in an image.

Most binoculars will also provide a third number, called the *field number*. This is the measurement, in degrees, of the area you'll see when looking through the binoculars. The bigger the number, the more you'll see.

Though your first reaction might be to jump at the 12x model, not only will it be more expensive, but objects will be harder to find, since, as magnification increases, brightness and field of view generally decrease. Binoculars that magnify 7x are more than sufficient.

For focusing, most binoculars have a central wheel that adjusts both eyepieces at the same time. Some models also have a dial around one of the eyepieces to adjust for a weaker eye.

identifying wildlife

At some point during your nature adventuring, you may wish to start identifying the wildlife you encounter by name. Here are some tips.

- Keep a written record of what you've observed. Include the date, time, weather, location, and elevation.

- Look for *field marks* on the animal you're observing. These are any color or pattern that can help identify an animal. Field marks include stripes, spots, streaks, bands or rings, a mask, or anything else that's easy to see, even from a distance.

- If observing a bird, look for streaks of color above the eyes, dark or light areas under the throat, neck rings, a crest or long head feathers.

- Watch how the animal walks, flies, or otherwise moves. A certain behavior can sometimes help figure out what it is.

- Write down what the animal is doing. You may have to watch the same animal several times before you can figure it out. You'll get better at noticing details each time you give it a try.

- If the animal is singing, howling, or making some other sort of noise, try to write down what the noise sounds like.

- Take a photograph or sketch the animal.

- Once you've gathered all your information and written down all your notes, it's time to consult a *field guide*, which is an illustrated book that provides good descriptions of plants or animals found in different habitats. Public libraries will have them available. Once you think you've found the animal you observed in the guide, add the name of the animal to your written record. Most guides will provide the animal's common name and two-part Latin name, its habitat, feeding preferences, breeding patterns, and more. Armed with this new information, you can go back to where you spotted this animal, and try to observe it again.

calling all animals!

For some reason, birds and other animals are attracted to squeaky calls. Why? Maybe they think you need help. Or, they think you're their next lunch. They may even simply be curious and want to get a closer look at the funny kid making all those silly noises.

a big "HEY YOU" animal call #1

WHAT YOU NEED

Long, wide blade of grass
2 craft sticks
Rubber band

1 Place the grass blade between the two sticks.

2 Wrap the rubber band around one end of the sticks.

3 With your fingers, pinch the end of the sticks without the rubber band, and blow. You should get a pretty cool sound. If you don't, try another piece of grass.

4 Once you've got a good, reliable sound, sit in your blind (see page 48), or simply go somewhere and be quiet, and blow into the contraption two or three times. Wait a few second, and try again and again and again. You may attract some curious birds or even a hungry fox.

a big "HEY YOU" animal call #2

This animal call should attract birds.

Make a loose fist, and hold it up to your mouth, so your thumb and curled-up index finger are facing you. Now put your lips together, press them to the fleshy part of your hand between your thumb and index finger (just below and behind the small opening between your index finger and palm), and make a long, loud, squeaky kiss noise. Wait a few seconds, then do it again, and again. Try a few short, high-pitched kisses, one right after the other. Or try a combination of long and short squeaks. Do the birds around you react differently to different kisses? With a little practice, you'll learn which kinds of squeaks attract the most birds.

a big "HEY YOU" animal call #3

This is another call that's good for birds.

Make a long, drawn-out "spish-h-h-h" sound three or four times in a row, like a shushing noise with an extra "sp" in front. Or try "pish-h-h-h." Do it over and over in a steady rhythm, and don't be shy about it. Good loud spishing often attracts all sorts of birds.

spish-h-h-h

walking and stalking

There may be times while hiking or camping when you'll luckily stumble upon something furry in a field 50 yards away—a deer, hare, or other really cool animal you've been dying to observe. Luckily, it didn't see you. It's time to stalk it.

WHAT YOU NEED

Binoculars (optional)

WHAT YOU DO

1 Since you want to get the best view of this creature, first figure out where the sun is, and walk around the animal until the sun's behind you.

2 Walk slowly, and get as close as you can. Go a little distance at a time, and stop for a few moments. Check out the animal with your binoculars. If you want to get closer, walk a few more steps. Try not to walk directly toward a bird—walk in a big semicircle around it.

3 If the ground is hard, put your toes down first. On soft ground, put your heels down first. Walk into the wind so your scent won't get picked up.

4 If the animal has seen you and seems jittery, stop and wait for it to calm down. Whatever you do, don't make any sudden movements.

5 The best time for stalking is early morning and late afternoon.

6 If you want to practice stalking, try out your technique on a house cat first.

stalked!

You and your friends can practice your stalking techniques with this fun game.

WHAT YOU NEED
4 or more friends
Blindfold
Water bottle or other object

WHAT YOU DO

1 Blindfold one participant and have him sit with the water bottle placed down in front of him.

2 Choose another participant to be a referee.

3 Everyone else is a potential stalker, whose job is to steal the water bottle away without the blindfolded person catching them.

4 Have the stalkers form a circle around the blindfolded person at least 12 feet away.

5 The referee then points to one stalker to sneak up and steal the bottle, while the blindfolded person concentrates on listening for potential stalkers.

6 If the blindfolded person hears something he points to the sound. The referee decides whether or not the blindfolded person caught the stalker.

7 If a stalker is caught, she must stay in the middle, and the referee points to the next stalker. The blindfolded person should get three chances to catch stalkers.

8 If a stalker grabs the bottle, she becomes the next blindfolded person. Don't forget to let everyone have a turn being blindfolded.

darn, i wish
i had my camera!

It happens all the time. You're out exploring, when suddenly you're face to face with the most amazing natural phenomenon ... and no camera. You don't need expensive camera equipment for nature photography. In fact, all you have to do is throw a small camera in your shirt pocket, and you're ready to go.

kinds of cameras

Read this section to see what kind of camera will fit your needs.

POINT-AND-SHOOT

These cameras take care of everything for you. All you need to do is aim and snap. Point-and-shoots use quality 35mm film, and they're lightweight, durable, and ready to use in a flash. On the downside, however, is that the viewfinder is separate from the lens, so what you see is not exactly what you get, which can cause problems with close-up shots. Also, the near-focus range is pretty limited, so if you get any closer than 2 or 3 feet, your picture will not come out.

SLR

Single-lens-reflex cameras (SLR) are more complicated than the point-and shoots (see photo on left). They're more powerful, and give you more control over what you're shooting. Also, when you look through the viewfinder of an SLR, you're looking through the actual lens of the camera, so what you see is exactly what you get. You can also change lenses, and they adjust to more types of lighting. Telephoto lenses can get you up close, while macro lenses can get you super close (great for insect shots). If you're serious about nature photography, this is the camera for you. Of course, it's significantly more expensive than a point-and-shoot, so if you're happy simply taking

taking great photos

good pictures, and you're not that interested in learning about photography, stick with the point-and-shoot.

DIGITAL

With digital cameras, you do not have to worry about film or processing. You can also print out your own photos or e-mail them right away.

DISPOSABLE

These are pretty much the same as point-and-shoot cameras, though the basic models don't have any sort of focus control.

Keep your camera steady by leaning it against a tree or other solid object. You could also use a tripod. An unsteady camera takes bad photos.

Another way to keep the camera steady is to sit down and brace your elbows on your knees. If you're using an SLR, place one hand under the lens.

Avoid taking photos around noontime on really sunny days. Colors will appear weak in your photographs. Try shooting on overcast days, if possible.

Take the same hike more than once so you're familiar with what you may be able to shoot. Camp yourself near a popular watering hole or a known animal home.

Be patient.

The best background is sky or water. Remember, animals tend to blend into their backgrounds.

Take tons of pictures. Even professionals use many rolls of film just to get a couple of good shots.

reading animal trails

Bear claw marks outside den entrances

FOOTPRINTS

Footprints are easy to find. Look around muddy puddles, streams, lakeshores, snowy fields, and wherever else the earth is soft.

What Can Footprints Tell You?

Footprints tell you the direction the animal was traveling.

The size of the footprints can give you a pretty good idea of the size of the animal.

If you see footprints in pairs, directly side by side, the animal is hopping or bounding like birds— it probably lives in a tree or bush.

In most cases the front footprints will be smaller than the rear ones.

Some animals, such as skunks, raccoons, beavers, porcupines, and bears, walk flat-footed. Foxes and bobcats walk on their toes. Deer walk on their hooves.

As animals move from one place to another, they usually leave a visible trail you can find if you look hard enough. Footprints, scratches, gnawed grass, and even droppings are just a few of the ways animals leave evidence that they were there. You can learn almost as much from animal trails as you can from the animals themselves.

OTHER SIGNS

Animal droppings tell you what the animal eats. Plant eaters leave pellet like droppings; whereas meat eaters' droppings are more cylinder shaped, and often contain fur hairs and bits of bones.

You might find cracked-open nuts, chewed grass, and other food leftovers.

Runways are well-worn paths, holes through hedges, and tunnels in long grass made by animals as they walk back and forth to water holes or feeding areas.

Snakes leave straight, unswerving, and zigzag curvy trails.

Stripped-away bark a few feet up a tree's trunk is evidence a deer was rubbing its antlers there.

Stripped-away bark at the base of a young tree's trunk could mean a mouse or rabbit was nibbling there.

Clumps of feathers may tell you an animal caught its dinner there.

Places where the ground has been scratched or dug up can mean a skunk or raccoon was looking for worms and grubs.

Many animals bite off and eat the ends of twigs and plant stems.

Sharp-toothed animals such as porcupines and rabbits leave a clean, angled bite mark; dear leave a torn, ragged edge.

casting tracks

Deer track

A muddy area is sometimes a great place to look for animal tracks. When you find some, cast the best-looking footprints for a long-lasting memento of your find.

WHAT YOU NEED

Half-gallon milk carton
Scissors
Plaster of paris
Water
Stick
Small shovel
Newspaper
Brush

WHAT YOU DO

1 Find clear animal tracks in mud or hard sand. Try to get one of each foot if possible, or at least a front and back.

2 Cut the carton in half with the top half cut into 1-inch rings.

3 Place the rings around the tracks, and push them carefully into the mud or sand.

4 In the bottom half of the carton, mix some plaster with a little bit of water until the mixture is the consistency of pancake batter (not too runny).

5 Gently pour the mixture into the rings.

6 Let the plaster harden in the molds for around one hour.

7 Carefully dig up the casts, and wrap them in newspaper.

8 Let the molds harden for several hours. Remove the carton rings, and clean the casts with water and a brush. (An old toothbrush works well.)

9 What you have now are the raised impressions of the tracks. You can use the cast to make tracks in clay if you like.

10 You may be able to cast the prints without the milk carton, though you'll still need a container.

TRACKS IN SNOW

If you want to preserve tracks in wet snow, sprinkle the tracks with dry plaster. Allow this to set. Then fill the track gently with the plaster of paris mixture. For dry snow, spray the track with water, allow it to freeze, and then fill with the plaster mixture. Or, simply dig around the print, lift it with a cake slicer or flat trowel, and pop it in a freezer. Once it's frozen solid you can make a cast out of it.

THE WAX METHOD

When the ground is dry, you may want to use this method. Light a candle, and drip wax into the print. Allow a rim of wax to form around the edge of the track as well as in the impression. Remove the wax when it's hard.

animal tracks

Here are several tracks you may encounter while hiking, camping, or simply exploring your backyard.

SQUIRREL

BEAVER

RABBIT

DEER

SKUNK

BEAR

RACCOON

DOG

CAT

FOX

bird restaurant

What do birds eat? Set the table and find out.

WHAT YOU NEED

5 or 6 terra cotta plant dishes
Choose 5 or 6 of the following
    foods: wild seed mixture,
    cheese, live worms, fat
    stripped from meat (wash
    your hands well after
    handling meat), dried fruit,
    bread crumbs, popcorn,
    and peanut butter

WHAT YOU DO

1 Place each food item on a different plate, and place the plates out in the open, preferably off the ground. A picnic table, large rock, or a wooden bench would work.

2 Watch to see who eats where. Take notes, and use a field guide to figure out what birds are eating what.

3 Experiment with other foods. Take tons of pictures if you want.

what can i eat with this beak?

Instead of a knife and fork, birds eat with their bills, and you can tell what a bird eats by observing its bill. They can act as chisels, hooks, spears, straws, and hammers. When bird watching, check to see if their bills match what they're eating.

Seed eaters such as cardinals and sparrows have short, strong, and thick bills for cracking seeds.

Woodpeckers have strong, long, chisel-like bills for creating holes in trees.

Hawks, owls, and eagles have sharp, curved bills for tearing meat.

Hummingbirds have long, straw-like bills that they use to sip nectar from flowers.

Insect eaters such as warblers and Western Meadowlarks have pointed, thin bills so they can reach into holes when grubbing for food.

Ducks have long, flat bills that strain plants and animals from the water.

Crows have a multi-purpose bill that allows them to eat just about anything they want, from fruit and seeds, to insects and fish.

Birds such as herons and kingfishers have spear-like bills for fishing.

CHAPTER FOUR

mini-wildlife

They make up three-quarters of the world's species. They're easy to find, and they don't usually mind being studied or even captured for a quick examination (as long as you let them go). And they're fun. We're talking about mini-creatures, or as most people call them: bugs. (Even mini-creatures that aren't bugs are usually called bugs anyway.) This chapter will get you up close and personal with the creeping, crawling insects, spiders, worms, centipedes, etc., while also showing you plenty of really cool ways of observing them without doing them any harm.

dress for bug success

When you're out there looking for bugs, there will be some bugs out there looking for you. Don't let the pests drive you back inside!

Hat

Bandanna
(to absorb sweat)

Long sleeves

Net

Long pants

Pants tucked into socks

Bug container

Sturdy shoes

OTHER TIPS

Use bug repellent. If you don't want to use a chemical spray, try a citrus- or herb-based repellent.

Mosquitoes are hungriest at dawn and dusk.

The light of a full moon will bring out more bugs.

If you get bitten, use an anti-itch ointment or cream, and avoid scratching it.

If you think you have a tick on you, have an adult remove it with a pair of tweezers, making sure the whole body is removed. Don't squeeze the tick, and swab the bite site with alcohol.

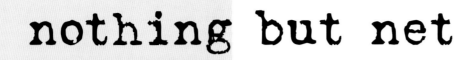

nothing but net

bug net #1

This net is perfect for sweeping back and forth in high grass in a field. It's also good for tennis practice.

WHAT YOU NEED

Old badminton or tennis racket
Scissors
Small, white, linen laundry bag with drawstring

WHAT YOU DO

1 Carefully remove the net from the racket with the scissors. Get an adult to help you.

2 Place the laundry bag around the hole of the racket.

3 Close the draw string around the hole.

4 Reach inside the bag, and pull it up back through the hole (turning it inside out).

bug net #2

This bug net is good for catching anything that happens to be flying around. Be careful with butterflies, since they have very fragile wings.

WHAT YOU NEED

Wire hanger
Tape measure
Tulle or other light
    netting material*
Scissors
Thick thread (quilter's
    thread works well)
Needle
Duct tape
Broom handle

* You can find tulle (a fine, silk or nylon netting that's usually used for veils, tutus, and gowns) at craft and fabric stores.

WHAT YOU DO

1 Straighten out the hanger's hook, and shape the triangular part of the hanger into a circle.

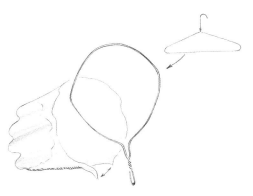

2 Measure the circumference of the circle, and cut a long rectangular piece of tulle in which two of the sides are about 2 inches longer than the circumference of the circle.

3 Position the tulle around the hanger until you've fashioned a tube with overlapping sides.

4 Sew the tulle to the wire hanger. Then, sew up the two overlapping sides, and wrap the bottom so there are no holes in the net. Get an older sibling or parent to help if you've never sewn anything before.

5 Attach the straightened hook of the hanger to the broomstick with duct tape. Keep rolling the tape over the spot until the net feels secure.

bug vacuum

If **you're trying** to collect small bugs that will be harmed if you attempt to use your fingers, create this cool vacuum, also known as a "pooter." Don't worry; you won't accidently swallow a fly.

WHAT YOU NEED

Clear plastic food container with top
Aquarium tubing
Scissors
Gauze
Small rubber band
Modeling clay

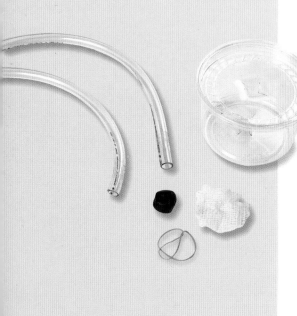

WHAT YOU DO

1 Poke a hole in the center of the lid with the scissors. Poke another hole in the center of the bottom of the container.

2 Cut the plastic tubing in half, and push each piece through the holes.

3 Remove the lid. With the rubber band, fasten the gauze over the end of the piece of tubing that will be inside the container.

4 Put the top back on the container.

5 Mold modeling clay around the tubes so that the holes they're in are airtight.

6 Find an insect small enough to fit in the tube, put your mouth on the tube with the gauze on it, place the other tube right up to the insect, and suck hard. The insect will be vacuumed into the container, and the gauze will prevent the bug from going up into your mouth.

insect viewer

Kids have been putting bugs in glass and plastic containers ever since glass and plastic containers were invented. Here's an improved version of the classic bug catcher.

WHAT YOU NEED
Hammer and nail
Plastic food jar with lid
Scissors or craft knife
Small magnifying glass
Scissors
Instant-bonding glue

WHAT YOU DO

1 Use the hammer and nail to make a circle of holes in the center of the lid.

2 Depending on how thick the lid is, use either the scissors or the craft knife to make a large hole in the center of the lid by cutting the material between the nail holes you made in step 1. The final hole should be a little smaller than the magnifying glass.

3 Poke some more holes along the edges of the lid.

4 Very carefully glue the outside edges of the magnifying glass to the lid. If the glue gets on the glass, quickly wipe it off with a wet rag.

5 Catch some bugs, and check them out.

Most likely, many of the insects you want to study live their lives out of sight, hidden in grass or under rocks and logs. One way to get a look at these shy creatures is to build a little trap, and let them come to you.

pitfall trap

WHAT YOU NEED

Trowel
Plastic food container
  with a wide mouth
4 rocks
Piece of plywood larger
  than the mouth of the
  food container

WHAT YOU DO

1 Dig a hole, and bury the jar so it's open end is even with the ground. Press the dirt down all around the jar right up to its rim.

2 Place the four rocks around the mouth of the container to hold the plywood roof.

3 Lay the board on top of the rocks. If the roof is over ½ inch above the mouth, use smaller rocks. The roof not only keeps the captive bugs from drowning when it rains, but also keeps birds from finding them before you do.

4 Place bits of cheese, bread, or fruit in the container, put the roof over the trap, and wait.

5 Check your trap every day, and let your captives go after examining them. Consider setting traps in different locations to see if you capture different bugs. When you're done, make sure you remove all your traps.

attracting ants

The next time ants invade your picnic or cookout, follow them, and see what they're up to.

First of all, how did all those ants find you? Ants communicate by smell. For example, once one ant realizes there's a food source (your lunch) nearby, it rushes back to its colony, releasing a scent trail all the way. Then, the worker ants simply follow the trail. If you notice a bunch of ants walking in a line (more or less) toward your granola bar or apple, try erasing the scent trail by rubbing across it with your finger. This will confuse the ants, and send them scurrying around trying to pick up the scent again.

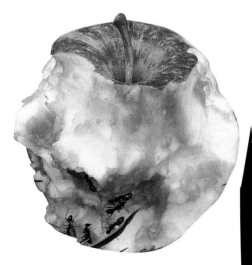

Leave some cookie crumbs by an ant hill, and watch them communicate and cooperate.

ANT FACTS

Ants live an average of eight years.

There are more ants on earth than any other creature.

We can lift about 60 percent of our weight. Ants can lift up to 50 times theirs. That's like you lifting an SUV.

If you step on an ant by mistake and crush its head, a chemical is released that informs ant soldiers nearby to get ready for a fight.

Ants produce a chemical that kills tiny pests, which is why you might see a bird let a bunch of ants

bug catching

If you take your catch inside for a day or two, place a damp (not too wet!), slightly balled-up paper towel in the jar with the bugs. The towel will give the bugs places to hide and something to drink. You could also use a damp sponge. Keep the towel or sponge moist with several drops of water daily.

Feed your bugs with leaves, fruit pieces, or whatever you happened to notice the bugs were eating when you caught them. If your captured bugs aren't eating anything, let them go after a day.

Watch out for bugs that sting, black spiders with a red hourglass shape on its underside (it's a black widow!), bees, wasps, big water bugs, or any beetle-like insect you find in water. If you don't know whether or not a bug is bad news, watch it all you want, but don't touch it.

collect a spider web

This activity will let you get a really good look at a spider web.

WHAT YOU NEED

Spider web
Black construction paper
  or board
White spray paint
Spray adhesive
Scissors
Spray acrylic sealer (optional)

WHAT YOU DO

1 Find a good web. Make sure its maker isn't home. Avoid any webs that have a spider's dinner in it or egg sacs, which look like small dust balls or cotton balls.

2 Spray the web with the white paint. Then, spray the paper or board with the adhesive, and quickly press it to the web without tearing it.

3 Cut the threads that are supporting the web.

4 If you want, spray the web and paper with a coat of spray acrylic sealer.

SPIDER FACTS

Unlike insects, spiders have two body parts. The first part is called the *prosoma*, and it contains the spider's eyes and mouth. The second is the *abdomen*, which is where the fluid that becomes the silk for its webs comes from.

The harvestman may look like a spider, but it's not. It has only one body part. Worldwide, there are 37 families of harvestmen. Members of only one family are properly referred to as "daddylonglegs."

Spider silk is stronger than steel wire of the same size.

butterfly or moth? you decide

It's easy to confuse moths and butterflies. They both flutter around with those cool wings, and they both sip nectar or water from flowers. Sure, moths have a reputation for being ugly, but look closely at a moth. Pretty cool, eh! If you want to tell the difference between moths and butterflies, read on.

? Butterflies have skinny antennae with knobs on the ends.

? Moths have feather-like antennae or thread-like antennae without knobs.

? When taking a break from flying, butterflies close their wings high above their backs, but can't fold them.

? Moths fold their wings down on top of their backs.

? Butterflies usually have long, slender bodies.

? Moths have fat, fuzzy bodies.

? Most butterflies rest during the night.

? Most moths rest during the day.

? Most moths spin a fluffy, silken cocoon when they get ready to change from a caterpillar.

? The pupal stage of a butterfly is spent in a smooth *chrysalis*.

earthworm apartment

The best way to observe a worm is to construct a "wormery" that will let you watch what worms do underground.

WHAT YOU NEED

Large glass or plastic container with lid
Garden soil
Decaying leaves
Sand
Water
Large rock (optional)
Leafy vegetable pieces
Cornmeal
3 or 4 earthworms
Piece of dark fabric
Black rubber band
Black construction paper

WHAT YOU DO

1 Fill the jar with alternate layers of garden soil, decaying leaves, and sand. Sprinkle each layer with a little water (don't soak), and try not to mix the layers. If you want to make sure to see worm tunnels, first place a rock in the middle of the jar before putting in the soil. This will force the worms to move toward the sides.

2 Make small pieces of the leafy vegetables and cornmeal your top layer.

3 Find three or four worms, and put them into the jar.

4 Since worms like it dark and damp, cover the top with the piece of dark fabric, and use the rubber band to secure it. Also use two or three rubber bands to secure the piece of construction paper around the outside of the jar.

5 Put the jar in a cool, dark place, and check it out every day. Make sure it's still damp in there, and take out any vegetables that have gone bad.

6 Wait for the worms to start tunneling and mixing the layers of soil. They'll also grab the vegetable leaf pieces into their burrow to eat. When you're finished checking out the worms, return them to their homes.

bee clock

Try this out in your yard or while camping. It's a great trick, and you can throw away your watch (just kidding).

WHAT YOU NEED
Small plate
Sugar water or cola
Watch

WHAT YOU DO

1 Set out a small plate of sugar water or cola somewhere outside.

2 When a couple of bees find the plate, note the time.

3 Do the same thing the next day at the same exact time.

4 On the third day, don't leave out the honey, but wait for the bees. Don't worry, they'll be right on time.

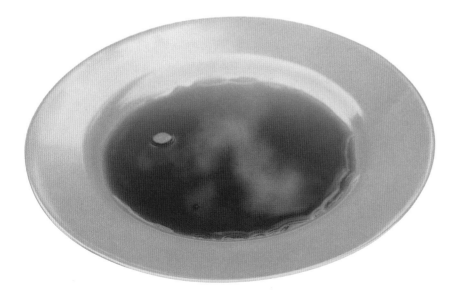

a bit about bees

✿ A bee's humming is made by the movement of its wings as it flies. As the wings vibrate, the air around them also vibrates, producing the buzzing noise that we can hear.

✿ A bee will roam up to three miles in search of food.

✿ Bees use the sun as a landmark.

✿ A bee who finds a food source will return to the hive and communicate where the food is by doing a little dance.

✿ Bees and plants seem to have a special agreement whereby everyone gets something. Bees get pollen and nectar from the flowers for food, and the flowers get accidently pollinated in return.

snail and slug detective

A little gross, perhaps, but definitely fascinating, these mini-creatures (called *gastropods*) are fun to explore, even if you don't want to touch them.

THE FACTS

Gastropoda (the class snails and slugs are in) means "stomach foot."

You can find them after it rains, in damp shady spots, or under logs. Slugs often come out at night when there's dew.

Snails and slugs have two pairs of antennae; the longer pair are eyes that can detect the difference between light and darkness, but little else.

They have a big open hole on one side of their bodies for breathing.

DUST FOR FOOTPRINTS

Mucous made by glands near the head forms a slimy cushion that hardens to form slime trails. This allows snails and slugs to move safely over sharp surfaces. They can also follow the trail to get back home.

Hunt for slime trails early in the morning. When you spot one, dust it lightly with powder to make it easier to follow.

MARK AND RECAPTURE

Snails frequently return to the same spot to rest. Look for a hideout; mark some snail shells with numbers or use a tiny dot of nail polish (don't touch the snail!); and see if they return.

BIG MUSCLES

A large foot runs the length of the snail and slug's body. When the muscles in this foot contract, they glide along. To get a clear view of the rippling muscle contraction that propels them forward, place a slug or snail on a sheet of glass or plastic or in a glass jar. Study the underside through the glass, and see the ripples push the snail forward from the tail end.

plant life

Plants are great to observe and study, especially since they don't move much, they rarely bite, and they don't hide. Plants are fascinating because they're one of the only life forms on this planet that can make their own energy. Everything else has to get its energy by eating plants, animals, or peanut butter and jelly sandwiches. Some plants are the oldest life forms on the planet, and just because they don't move doesn't mean they aren't clever. You can determine climates of the past by studying tree rings, make a leaf tell you what it does, unwittingly plant some seeds, read lichen for signs of pollution, and more.

pocket sketchbook

This easy-to-make book can go with you just about anywhere and is perfect for sketching wildflowers, trees, and landscapes.

WHAT YOU NEED

Piece of corrugated
  cardboard, 5 x 11 inches
10 to 12 sheets of drawing
  or writing paper, each
  4¾ x 10½ inches
Large nail
Long piece of string
Scissors
Cardboard tube
Craft knife
Tape
Short pencil or pen

WHAT YOU DO

1 Roll up the cardboard until you have fat roll that's 5 inches tall. Unroll it and fold it in half.

2 Fold the sheets in half, and slip them inside the cardboard cover.

3 With the nail, poke three holes through the cardboard and paper in the fold of the book, about 1 inch apart.

4 Enlarge the holes with the nail until they're big enough to thread the string through.

5 Pass the string through the center hole. Then pass it up through the top hole. Pass it down through the bottom hole. Then, up through the center hole. Pull the string ends tight. Tie a bow at the center hole, and trim the ends.

6 With the craft knife, cut the tube a little bit taller than the book's height.

7 For the pencil sleeve, cut two pieces of tape 2 inches long. Lay them sticky side up on a tabletop. Put a 1-inch piece of tape in the center of each strip to make a sort of tape bandage. Tape one end of the first piece of tape to the tube. Hold up the other end of the bandage, and place the pen or pencil under the part of the bandage that's not sticky. Pull the bandage over the pencil, and stick down the other end. Repeat this step with the other tape bandage. You should be able to slide the pencil in and out.

8 Drawing animals, insects, and plant life is a neat way to explore nature. It helps us remember what we see. Don't think you have to be an artist to sketch. Simply draw what you see, and if it's not worthy of Michelangelo, well, who cares? When sketching something that might fly or run away, make an outline sketch first, and jot down some quick notes about its appearance so you can keep drawing after it takes off.

how old is that tree?

The only accurate way to find out a tree's age is to cut it down. Accurate, but not great for the tree. The following method will not only give you a good estimate of a tree's age, but will also let the tree keep aging.

WHAT YOU NEED
Tape measure
Tree

WHAT YOU DO

1 Use the tape measure to figure out the circumference of the tree trunk.

2 Trees have an average growth of 1 inch per year, so if you measured 35 inches, the tree may be around 35 years old.

dendrochronology

Dendrochronology is a form of science that studies time through trees.

A tree grows from spring until fall. Every year, it adds a new growth ring. When a tree ring is thick, scientists know that it was a good year for growing, which usually means it was a wet summer. If it's narrow, the tree couldn't get enough water to grow very much that year. A tree grows a new ring for every year it's alive.

Scientists use dendrochronology to find out about climate changes long ago. They use this information to make predictions about what's happening with our climate. Dendrochronology is also used to figure out how old archaeological sites near trees are.

Do this activity with a tree that has recently fallen. If camping or hiking, ask a park ranger or camp official if she knows of any recently fallen trees.

WHAT YOU NEED

Fallen tree or dead wood that has been cut open
Magnifying glass
Tape measure

WHAT YOU DO

1 If you can't find someone who can tell you of any recently felled trees, pick a trail that you know is regularly maintained. Hike it a week or so after a major storm, since the storm may have blown some old trees down. You'll probably find a few that fell on the trail. If the clean-up crew has been through, they will have cut these trees in half and pushed them to the side of the path. This is the perfect opportunity to do a little dendrochronology.

2 Using your magnifying glass and tape measure, count how many rings are on the tree. Where are the growth rings different sizes? Does the tree have any unusual scars?

3 Figure out the year the tree was planted, and if you're really interested, figure out which years were good for the tree's growth, and which ones weren't. You can ask grandparents and parents if they remember those years. What was the weather like during those years when the rings were very narrow?

my, how tall you are!

Sure, you could measure a tree with a really long tape measure and a helicopter, but with a little math, it's a bit easier to figure out the height of a tree using only a ruler and a piece of chalk.

WHAT YOU NEED

Ruler
Piece of chalk

WHAT YOU DO

1 Use the ruler to measure 5 feet from the ground on the trunk of the tree. Mark the spot with the chalk.

2 Hold the ruler at eye level with your arm outstretched. Shut one eye and back away from the tree (carefully) until the bottom 5 feet of the tree trunk appears to be the same length as the bottom ½ inch space on your ruler.

3 Measure the height of the tree in inches. Multiply the number of inches by 10, and you'll get the height of the tree in feet. (If ½ inch equals 5 feet, then each inch equals 10 feet.)

got a favorite tree?

🌲 Photograph it at the same time every year. Or have someone take a picture with you in front of it every year.

🌲 Dry some leaves from your tree, and paint miniature paintings on them.

bark and leaf rubbings

How do you impress a tree? Leaf it alone! Really, don't pull bark off a tree; instead, try this activity, and put your rubbings in the notebook on page 91 if you wish.

WHAT YOU NEED

Trees
Hard surface, such as a notebook or a hardcover book
Unlined paper
Wax crayons

WHAT YOU DO

1 Gather some leaves that have fallen from different types of trees. Make sure you get leaves that are not too brown or brittle.

2 Place the leaves on the hard surface. Put the piece of paper on top of them and gently press the paper down to spread them out.

3 Peel the paper wrapper off the crayon. Rub the side of the crayon back and forth across the paper while pressing down. You'll start to see an impression of the leaf on your paper. Keep the pressure even, and stop rubbing when you can see the whole leaf on your paper. Do this for every leaf you have.

4 For bark rubbings, tape a sheet of paper to the trunk of a tree. Rub the crayon back and forth over the paper. You'll get an impression of the tree bark on your paper.

5 Match each leaf with the bark of the tree it came from.

6 Make your own tree book, or add your impressions to your journal. Use a field guide to identify your tree. Write the name of the tree and the day you found it below your rubbings.

7 You can also turn rubbings into creative art projects. Make cards, gift wrap, book covers, party invitations, or anything you might use paper for.

bag a leaf

food factories

Leaves are plants' food factories. First, plants collect water through their roots. They also take carbon dioxide from the air. Then, a chemical in the leaves called *chlorophyll* (which gives the leaves their green color) absorbs from sunlight the energy that is used in transforming carbon dioxide and water to *glucose*, a kind of sugar plants use as food for energy and growing. (This process is called *photosynthesis*.) If there's extra water after the process, it's the leaves' job to get rid of it, which is why you may have found moisture in the bag.

What do leaves do? Bag one and find out.

WHAT YOU NEED
Healthy plant
Clear plastic bag
Tape

WHAT YOU DO

1 Put the bag over one of the leaves on the plant. Seal the bag up with the tape. Be careful not to stick the tape to the plant.

2 Go away for a few hours.

3 Come back, remove the bag, and see how much moisture has accumulated.

4 Repeat the activity, but this time do it with a deciduous tree (a tree that loses its leaves in the fall) and a coniferous tree. Leave the bags on for the same amount of time. Which tree gives off more water?

identifying leaves

Leaves come in many shapes or sizes, with each different type of leaf providing plants with optimun sunlight exposure. Scientists use leaves to help identify plant species.

THE PARTS OF A LEAF:

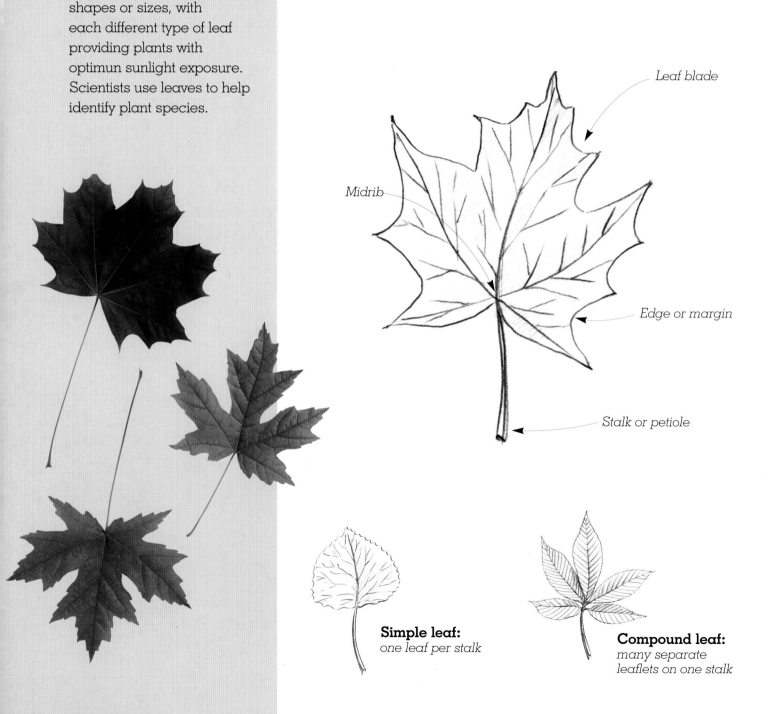

Leaf blade

Midrib

Edge or margin

Stalk or petiole

Simple leaf:
one leaf per stalk

Compound leaf:
many separate leaflets on one stalk

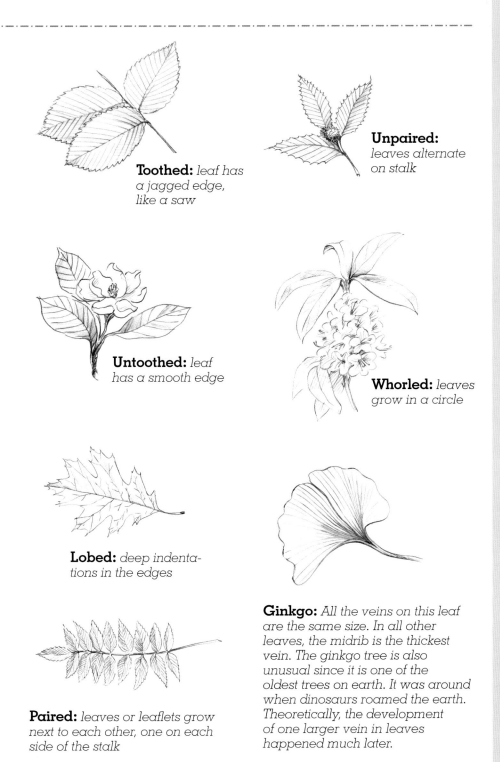

Toothed: *leaf has a jagged edge, like a saw*

Unpaired: *leaves alternate on stalk*

Untoothed: *leaf has a smooth edge*

Whorled: *leaves grow in a circle*

Lobed: *deep indentations in the edges*

Paired: *leaves or leaflets grow next to each other, one on each side of the stalk*

Ginkgo: *All the veins on this leaf are the same size. In all other leaves, the midrib is the thickest vein. The ginkgo tree is also unusual since it is one of the oldest trees on earth. It was around when dinosaurs roamed the earth. Theoretically, the development of one larger vein in leaves happened much later.*

why fall happens

Deciduous trees lose their leaves in the fall. If they tried to keep their leaves all year round, the tree would die of thirst. As you saw in the last activity, leaves give off a lot of water. In the winter, the water underground is frozen, and the tree can't get to it. So every fall the tree absorbs all of the water and food in its leaves into its branches and trunk. Then it grows a corky layer in between the twig and the stem of the leaf. Eventually the leaf falls off. Now the tree can live happily on the water it has stored inside of itself.

Evergreens don't drop their needles since they don't lose nearly as much water as deciduous trees.

the clever world of seeds

The world is full of seeds, and although they can't move, plants are very good at getting you and other animals to take them where they need to go. They do this through seed dispersion.

There are four types of seed dispersion:

Wind. Dandelions, thistles, maple trees, and many other plants spread their seeds this way. The seeds are light, and have a sail to catch the wind. Because these plants have no control over where the wind takes their seeds, they produce far more than they need.

Animals. Some plants, like burdocks, have developed ways for their seeds to stick to passing animals (people too!). The animals carry the seeds far away. Other plants hide their seeds in fruits and berries. When animals eat the fruit, they eat the seed as well. These seeds have special shells that keep the seed from being digested. When the animal poops out the seed, it's far from home and in a nice bed of fresh manure.

Water. Many seeds are developed to float from one place to another. The most famous example is the coconut seed, which can float hundreds of miles across the sea.

Expulsion. A few plants have figured out how to fling their seeds away from them when an animal brushes up against them. Touch-me-nots, poppies, and the squirting cucumber all do this.

a seedy experiment

Put big socks over your shoes. Take a walk through some high grass or bushes. Take off the socks, and shake off all of the seeds that stuck to you over a piece of white paper. Sort the seeds by type. Look at them under a magnifying glass. Can you see how they attached to you? Plant them and see what comes up.

WHAT ARE THE BIRDS EATING? ANOTHER SEEDY EXPERIMENT

Birds plant a lot of seeds. Plants hide their seeds in delicious fruits and berries for the birds to eat. The birds eat the seeds along with the fruit. Then, the seeds pass through the birds' digestive tracts and are planted with a nice coating of organic materials (bird poop). Find some bird poop. Get a small shovel, and dig up the dropping without touching it. Plant it somewhere. Wash your hands. After the seeds come up, see what kind of plants that bird was eating.

SOME INTERESTING SEEDS

- The pinecones of a jack pine are sealed shut. They'll only open if they're burned. That sounds a little weird, doesn't it? They do this because after a forest fire has passed through, all of the plants on the ground have been killed. There is no competition for the jack pine seeds on the forest floor, so they get a head start on all of the other plants.

- Chocolate comes from the seeds of a cocoa plant.

- The largest seed in the plant kingdom is the coco de mer, or double coconut palm; it weighs 60 pounds.

pressing flowers

A good way to preserve the flowers you collect is to press them. You can stick them between the pages of a fat textbook, but this contraption is easier to carry around.

WHAT YOU NEED

2 pieces of wooden board
 (10 x 12 inches or smaller
 is a good size)
Several pieces of cardboard,
 same size as the boards
1 or 2 belts
Several sheets of white
paper

WHAT YOU DO

1 Place the cardboard pieces between the two wooden boards.

2 Place the two belts around the cardboard "sandwich," and tighten the belts. Make sure the belts are easily adjustable.

3 As you find flowers or leaves, place them between sheets of white paper, and sandwich them between the cardboard. Tighten the belts.

4 Take the pressed flowers out after a few weeks. Put your dried plant life in your journals, or create neat cards, pictures, collages, or bookmarks.

Note: Only collect flowers if you're allowed to do so. Many wildflowers are endangered species and can't afford to be plucked for your collection. Always ask first. And, when in doubt, sketch the flowers you find instead.

plant life journal

This combination journal/sketchbook/collector's book is fun to make, and it's great for identifying the plant life you come across on walks and hikes.

WHAT YOU NEED

Blank journal with
    unlined pages
Several envelopes with clasps
Scissors
Tape
Small self-sealing
    plastic bags
Jute string
Glue
Bead (optional)
Thick ribbon
Hook-and-loop tape

WHAT YOU DO

1 Cut the envelopes so they fit in the book. Make them different sizes if you want, and if you're cutting larger envelopes, don't be afraid to cut up to three sides of the envelope so that it fits. Simply tape the cut sides closed to create personalized envelopes.

2 Tape small self-sealing plastic bags in the book for seed collecting.

3 Cut a piece of string long enough to wrap around the spine of the book.

4 Glue one end of the string along the outside edge of the book, and let it come down through the pages of the book for a bookmark. Attach a bead at the other end of the string if you wish.

5 Cut the ribbon so it's about 4 inches longer than the front and back cover of the book. Glue it to the middle of the covers so that the back end of the ribbon comes around up to the front of the book.

6 Attach a strip of heavy-duty hook-and-loop tape between the two edges of ribbon so the ribbon becomes a good way to keep the book closed. Your book's now ready to go exploring with you.

a close encounter with death and decay

Dead trees provide food, shelter, and nesting sites for many forest creatures. Trees collect minerals and nutrients from the surrounding soil and air as they grow. When a tree dies, these nutrients are available to other plants and animals. The decaying log leaves behind a rich, dark layer of soil called *humus*. Take a close look at who's taking advantage of this wonderful situation.

WHAT YOU NEED

A fallen tree or large limb
Magnifying glass
4 or 5 jars with lids
  with holes in them
Pencil
Notebook
Field guides to insects
  and spiders (optional)

WHAT YOU DO

1 Find a large fallen tree limb or large log in the woods. Examine the log with the magnifying glass, and try to find at least one creature from each of these areas: on top of the log, under the bark, underneath the log or on the ground nearby. Don't stick your bare hand into dark holes. Use a small stick to move things around instead.

2 Put the creatures in a jar to look at them more closely. Draw them in your notebook, and write down what part of the tree you found them on. Do you notice any insects or other creatures that are found throughout the log? Are others in just one place? Which insects are feeding on the log? What's eating the insects feeding on the log? Look for evidence of nesting sites. Do you see any larvae that might be feeding on the wood? Are there any plants growing out of the log? Do you see any molds or fungi? When you're finished studying them, put them back where you found them.

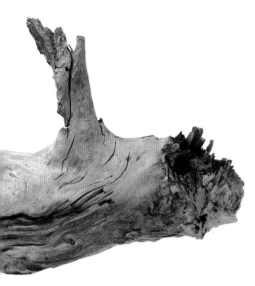

3 Use field guides to help identify the insects and spiders if you want.

4 If you live near this site, come back every month and record your findings. Does the log have more creatures? Note the changes to the wood and amount of humus that has formed. Record how long it takes for the log to completely decay.

 A decaying log can house 20,000 creatures.

One-third of all forest species live in fallen trees, from chipmunks and salamanders, to carpenter ants, fungi, and woodlice.

lichen the pollution spotter

Lichen is a tough little plant that can be found growing in all sorts of inhospitable climates: on bare rock, in deserts, even in the Arctic and Antarctic. There is only one place lichen won't grow: where there's too much air pollution. Lichens are particularly sensitive to *sulfur dioxide*, which is an emission created by power plants, large industrial facilities, electricity, and cars.

Lichen is actually made up of two different plants that have a *symbiotic* relationship, which means that both plants benefit from their relationship. Algae cells grow in the middle of fungus. The algae performs photosynthesis and feeds the fungus. In turn, the fungus supports and shelters the algae.

Lichen don't have roots; they absorb all of their nutrients directly from rainwater. Soil filters many pollutants from being absorbed by regular plants, but lichen can't. It will continue to absorb sulfur until the sulfur breaks down the chlorophyll molecules that perform photosynthesis. Then, the algae dies, and the fungus starves to death soon after.

Study the lichen you find on your nature adventures. The greener the lichen, the healthier the air you're breathing.

did you pack the predators?

People have been moving plants from one area of the world to another for quite some time now. These new plants have an unfair advantage over the existing plants: no competition. The native plants have other plants, insects, and animals to keep their growth in check, but the new plant left all those things behind. It can grow as much as it wants, and nothing will stop it. That's why these plants are called *invasive* plants.

Eventually, an invasive plant will grow so much it monopolizes all of the soil and sunlight, leaving no room for the native plants to grow.

Unfortunately, the animals that ate the native plants can't just start eating the invasive plant. They either starve to death or move. A single invasive plant can drastically change an entire ecosystem.

Kudzu was introduced to America from Japan in 1876 and was promoted as a good solution to soil erosion. The vine grows as much as a foot a day and does not hesitate to cover over everything in its path (see photo). It grows over plants, fences, trees, telephone poles, buildings, and whatever else stands still long enough to be covered. Kudzu now covers more than 7 million acres of land in the southern United States, and it's hard (nearly impossible) to get rid of.

fun plant facts

- A single rye plant can spread as much as 400 miles of roots.

- At mid-summer, the leaves of the compass plant point precisely north and south.

- Squirrels plant trees by forgetting where they put their stash.

- Plant pollen is highly flammable. It was used in the very beginning of modern theater for artificial lighting.

- The biggest, stinkiest flower is the *rafflesia*—it's 3 feet across and smells like rotting meat. The smell attracts the insects that will pollinate it.

explore the shore

You're most likely to visit a shoreline or bank during a family vacation, whether it's a creek, pond, stream, lake, or ocean. Each different shore supports unique life forms, and this chapter gives you the tools to explore any or all of the bodies of water you may encounter, and the plants and animals that make these water habitats their home. Figure out how fast a creek is moving; find out what's swimming around at night; learn to skip stones; observe what the oceans' tides leave behind; and more.

waterscope

Here's a contraption you can make in about five minutes that will let you get close to what's going on underwater without getting all wet. Although great for a small stream or creek, it can also be used to view underwater ocean and pond activity.

WHAT YOU NEED
Plastic container, such as
   a milk jug or tennis
   ball container
Scissors or craft knife
Heavy-duty plastic wrap
Rubber band
Duct tape

WHAT YOU DO

1 Cut off the bottom of the container.

2 Stretch a piece of plastic wrap over the bottom hole in the container, and hold it in place with the rubber band. Adjust the plastic so there are no wrinkles.

3 Wrap a piece of duct tape around the rubber band to further secure the plastic.

4 To use the scope, press it underwater so that the water comes up the side of the container but not into it. Peer down through the top. The water slightly magnifies things, so everything you see will look just a little bit larger.

water exploring safety tips

Never explore a stream, creak, tide pool, etc. alone. It's best to have an adult with you. Even shallow water can be deceptively dangerous.

Don't lean too far out over any body of water. You might fall in.

Watch out for slippery rocks, logs, when walking in and around streams, ponds, and tide pools.

Consider wearing shoes when wading through water.

Don't attempt to pick up any animal you're not 100 percent sure about.

Don't pick up anything in the water that looks like a beetle.

sifting screen

3 Scoop up some stream mud or ocean sand, place it on top of the screen, shake the screen a bit, and use your hand to rub the mud or sand back and forth over the screen. You can also dip the screen in the water to help drain the mud or sand.

Check out what's in the sand or the mud by the water. You might find some cool-looking rocks, a strange bug or two, shells, and maybe even something you can't identify at all!

WHAT YOU NEED

Window screen
Scissors
Picture frame
Heavy-duty staple gun
    and staples

WHAT YOU DO

1 Cut a piece of window screen big enough to fit over the picture frame.

2 Place the screen over the opening in the frame, and staple one side of it to the frame. Stretch the screen across the frame, and staple the opposite side to the frame. Then, staple the other two ends.

how fast is your creek moving?

A stream's velocity (speed) is important in keeping wildlife healthy by providing oxygen to the water. The more oxygen, the greater the variety of aquatic insects. You'll need a partner (and an adult) to help you with this fun orange race.

WHAT YOU NEED

Twine or string
Orange
Stopwatch
Tape measure
Notebook and pencil

WHAT YOU DO

1 Pick a spot in the creek where the water's flowing at a steady rate. Make sure there aren't a lot of large logs or rocks to stop your orange in this section.

2 Now it's time to get wet! (Make sure you wear shoes in the creek because sharp objects like broken glass and fishing hooks often cannot be seen.) Don't walk into a creek you're unfamiliar with, and have an adult check out the current before you get in. Don't try this with a deep, fast-moving river!

3 Choose a start and finish line at least 15 to 20 feet apart. Stretch the twine across the creek from one side to the other just above the surface of the water at the start and finish lines. Measure the exact distance between the start and finish lines with the tape measure. Record this distance in your notebook.

4 Stand in the creek at the start line, and have your partner wait in the creek at the finish line with the stopwatch.

5 Drop the orange into the water just upstream from the start line. When the orange floats past the start line, yell "start!" Your partner then begins timing the orange with the stopwatch. When the orange crosses the finish line, your partner stops the watch, catches the orange, and records the time in seconds in the notebook.

6 If the orange gets trapped by debris or rocks, start over.

STREAM VELOCITY CHART

7 Repeat the orange race nine more times. You can make a table to record the times like the one on the right, or make your own.

8 To find out the average velocity or speed of your creek, you must first find the average time it took for your orange to float from start to finish. Add together all the times (in seconds), and then divide that sum by 10 (ex., 33 + 33 + 31 + 27 + 32 + 31 + 30 + 28 + 25 + 30 = 300. 300/10 = 30 seconds). Now, divide the distance between the start and finish lines by the average time (ex. 15 feet/30 seconds = 0.50 feet/second). So, in this example, it took 1 second for the orange to move ½ foot or 6 inches.

Distance = _____ feet

Trial #	Time (in seconds)
1	_____
2	_____
3	_____
4	_____
5	_____
6	_____
7	_____
8	_____
9	_____
10	_____
Total	_____

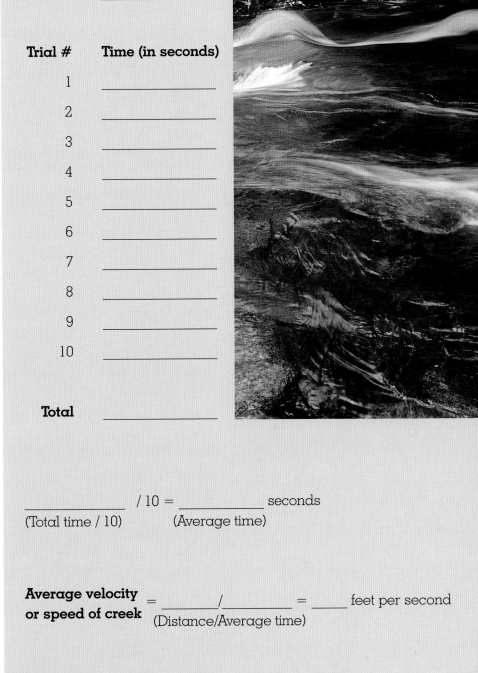

_____ / 10 = _____ seconds
(Total time / 10)   (Average time)

Average velocity or speed of creek = _____/_____ = _____ feet per second
(Distance/Average time)

Go out before it rains and then the day after, and compare the two rates.

all about beavers

Beavers and people are two of the only mammals that shape their environment to make it easier to live, work, and play in. Beavers don't use backhoes, dump trucks, and concrete, however. They use their sharp, strong teeth to cut down trees to make their dams and lodges. Then they gather armfuls of rocks and mud to fill in the gaps between the logs. Beavers build watertight dams because they like to live in deep water, where they have plenty of room to swim, dive, and play.

After they finish building the dam, they work on the lodge, which looks like a big pile of sticks above water. The entrances are underwater, but the living spaces are above water. When the water freezes, beavers spend all winter in their lodges.

Beavers build, and when they're done building, they constantly improve their lodges and dams. What keeps beavers as busy as a ... well ... beaver? Believe if or not, the simple sound of running water makes them do it. Perhaps, they think the running water means one of their structures has sprung a leak. Beavers also build constantly because, like all rodents, their teeth never stop growing, and they need to keep them worn down.

Eventually, the beaver family will use up all of the trees where it lives. When this happens, they move to a new place and start over. The dam breaks down eventually, and the water drains out. The soil that is left behind is very rich and fertile and will soon become a meadow for different plants and animals.

SIGNS OF BEAVER ACTIVITY

 Clearings around streams and lakes

 A dam

 A lodge (see photo on page 100). (Don't ever step on a beaver lodge! Adult beavers weigh as much as a medium-size dog, have teeth as strong as a chainsaw, and wouldn't take kindly to your crashing through their ceiling.)

 Webbed tracks and tail marks

 Tree stumps chewed into points

Trees that have been debarked

The loud slap of a tail hitting water (This means the beaver saw you and is warning its family to stay undercover.)

night light

Spending the night close to a river, lake, pond, marsh, or ocean? Take a peak at what's going on after hours with this easy-to-make night light.

WHAT YOU NEED

Flashlight with
    fresh batteries
Self-sealing plastic bag
Clear container with lid
    (big enough to
    hold flashlight)
Rock or something heavy

WHAT YOU DO

1 Turn on the flashlight, place it in the plastic bag, and seal the bag.

2 Place the bag along with the rock into the jar. Seal the jar with its lid.

3 Tie the string around the neck of the jar. Make sure the string won't slip off the container.

4 Stand or kneel on a boardwalk, dock, or just on the bank, and lower the night-light into the water. Check out who's attracted to your light, and for a closer inspection, use the net on page 69 to scoop out a critter or two. Don't forget to put them back.

skipping stones

It's easiest to skip stones in a pond or lake. It's fun to learn, and it's also fun finding the perfect rocks to skip.

WHAT YOU NEED
Body of water
Several flat rocks

WHAT YOU DO

1 Find a body of water. Find a bunch of flat rocks, smaller than the palm of your hand. The rocks don't have to be circular.

2 Standing at the bank, pick up one of the rocks, and hold it in your hand with your index finger wrapped around the stone. The stone should be between your middle finger and thumb.

3 Wind up by swinging your arm back and lowering your hand toward the water. Release the rock by throwing sidearm as fast as you can, and snap or flick your wrist to release the stone. The stone should spin off the end of your finger. If the stone hits parallel to the water's surface, you may get a good run. This is one sport that's fun to practice.

STONE SKIPPING TERMINOLOGY

Plinks: the clean beginning skips at the beginning of a rock's skipping.

Pitty-pats: short skips at the end of a rock's run.

Crest-out: a rock that hits a wave and shoots up into the air instead of skipping.

Plonk: a rock that sinks without skipping at all.

beach exploring

another whole world you didn't know existed.

Bring some large self-sealing plastic bags with you in order to examine what you find. They work better than pails. Simply place the ocean critter in the bag with some water. Watch it for a while, and then return it where you found it. You can also bring a sifting screen (see page 97), a small shovel, a bag for collecting abandoned shells, a waterscope (see page 96), and a pair of binoculars.

A vacation to the beach is a time for swimming, applying sunscreen, making sandcastles, and getting sand in your shorts. But it's also a great time to explore nature. Look a little closer. What animals do you see? What are they doing? Are there any tide pools nearby?

After a day at the beach, come back at night with an adult. Bring a flashlight covered with red cellophane, and see what's going on after all the sunbathers leave for the day. If you get there as the tide's retreating, you might find

ocean shore facts

WHAT IS SAND?

Sand is ground-up rocks and shells. How did the rocks and shells get that way? Waves pulled them into the water, where, over the course of thousands of years, the rocks and shells scraped and tumbled against each other, breaking into smaller and smaller pieces, until they became grains of sand.

WHAT CAN YOU FIND IN THE SAND?

Place some beach sand in a strainer or sifter (see page 97), and see what remains once the sand has passed through. You may find small shells, pebbles, and even fish teeth.

WHAT MAKES WAVES BREAK?

When a wave approaches the shore, the bottom of the wave drags against the seabed, slowing it down, while the top of the wave keeps going at the same speed until it falls over and crashes onto the beach.

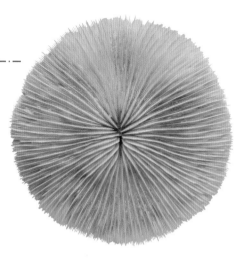

WHAT CAUSES TIDES?

In a word, gravity. Even though the world's oceans are kept in place by earth's gravitational pull, the gravity of the moon (and sun) tugs at the oceans and pulls them up. High tide occurs when ocean water reaches its highest point on the coast. Low tide is when ocean water reaches its lowest point on the coast. High and low tide usually happen twice each day at different times.

WHERE DOES THE SALT IN OCEAN WATER COME FROM?

All of the world's rivers carry the salt contained in dirt and rocks to the oceans. When water in the ocean evaporates, the salt is left behind.

observe a tidal pool

Tidal pools are pockets or pools of ocean left behind on the coasts after high tide recedes. Some are merely puddles in the sand, while others are large, deep pools between rocks that can sustain an interesting community of life.

If the beach you're visiting has tide pools, ask a lifeguard, park ranger, or other beach official if it's okay to explore it.

What will you find? While exploring, you may find algae, snails, barnacles, sand dollars, starfish, and crabs. Think of these animals as survivors that must withstand waves, rocks, and the possibility of their home drying out before the tide comes in again.

Remember that rocks with seaweed on them are quite slippery, making rocky shores dangerous places to investigate. Always wear shoes with good traction, and explore with a friend.

Always tell adults where you're going.

Don't touch a sea urchin's spines, and don't touch a jellyfish, even if it's dead.

Don't get cut off by the tide.

Replace any rocks you turn over.

Don't pull off algae or animals that are attached to rocks.

Don't take shells from a tide pool. They may provide needed protection for some animals.

beach combing

The shells you are most likely to find while beach-combing come from mollusks, the largest group of shelled animals.

A clam is a *bivalve*, the same as oysters, mussels, and scallops. Bivalves have two shells, and there are over 35,000 species of bivalves known to scientists.

The other kind of shell you'll find is a *gastropod* or snail. They only have one shell, often in a spiraled shape. There are more than 40,000 species of sea gastropods.

Here are some shells you might find on a beach. See how many you can identify, and consult a field guide for the ones you can't.

dig for clams

By the way, if you're wading in the ocean one day, and see a snail shell moving swiftly, you may not be looking at the world's fasted snail, but a hermit crab. They live in unoccupied shells. And when they get too big for the shell they borrowed, they simply find a bigger one.

Look for tiny holes at the water's edge. These holes may mean there are clams hiding below. Clams dig themselves into the sand with a strong muscle called a foot. (It doesn't look like a foot!) Once it's deep enough and feels safe, it stretches a pair of long siphons up to the surface of the sand. Food (plant and animal particles) and water pour into one of these tubes when the waves come in. The clam squirts the unneeded water out through the other tube. When danger is near or if the tide is out, clams pull in their siphons and "clam up" by tightly closing their shells.

If you want to see a clam in action, dig carefully around where you saw those tiny holes. If you do find a clam, watch it for awhile, but leave it there. Clams hold themselves pretty tightly down there, and if you try to take one out, you may break its shell. Plus, it's probably happy where it is.

seaweed facts

WHAT IS SEAWEED?

Though called weeds, the many plants found growing in oceans are really marine algae. Some marine and freshwater algae can only exist as single cells, but seaweed is much bigger and can be seen without a microscope. Most seaweed attach themselves to rocks and shells, though sometimes you may see them floating in the water.

EDIBLE SEAWEED

Seaweed ice cream? You bet. Look at the ingredient list of your favorite foods. If you see the words *carrageenan, alginin, agar,* or *furcellaran,* you're eating extracts of seaweed. Here's a list of just some of the products with seaweed in them: salad dressing, milk shakes, sherbets, instant pudding, cottage cheese, whipped cream, yogurt, soft drinks, fruit juice, bakery goods, candy, sauces, baby food. Also, toothpaste, shampoo, air freshener, shaving cream, cough medicine, shoe polish, and even canned pet food.

SEAWEED FORECAST

Want to know what the weather is going to be? Take a few long pieces of seaweed, and hang them upside down from a fence or tree. Several hours later, touch the seaweed. If the air is moist, the seaweed will soak up the moisture, and it will feel wet. Rain may be on the way. If the air is dry, the air will absorb moisture from the seaweed, drying it. This means there is probably no rain in the forecast.

night life

Night isn't simply the absence of the sun. It's a time when our imaginations take over—when an owl screeching can raise the hairs on your neck, or a simple campfire story involving a couple of ghosts and goblins can make you wish you had your teddy bear with you. And just because *you* sleep at night doesn't mean everything else does as well. In fact, night is the preferred time for many of the world's animals to wake up and start their day. The activities in this chapter will keep you up past your bedtime investigating the world that wakes up after the sun goes down. So, grab a flashlight, gather up some friends, and prepare to adjust your senses as you slowly become a night animal yourself.

night hike

Hiking at night can be a unique experience. You might hear and even see things that are usually sleeping and hiding during the day.

WHAT YOU NEED

An adult partner
Flashlight
Red plastic acetate (available at photography supply stores) or red cellophane
Rubber band

WHAT YOU DO

1 Choose a trail that you know well during the day. Make sure night hiking is allowed on the trail you're planning to use. Don't night hike alone, and always bring an adult with you.

2 Tape the red plastic over the flashlight so only red light shines through when you turn it on.

3 Let your eyes adjust to the darkness for at least 10 minutes before beginning the hike.

4 Begin your night hike using your red flashlight. Your chances are better of seeing night animals if you hike as quietly as possible so you don't alarm them. Even if you see nothing, listen carefully. Nocturnal animals, such as owls, are very quiet. However, if you try to "hoot" like an owl, you may be surprised to hear one calling back. Owls are territorial and communicate their boundaries with calls.

5 Go back to the same trail in the morning, and look for evidence of nocturnal animals that may have been nearby.

get out your night eyes

my, what big retinas you have

Go outside at night, and after five minutes in the dark, use a flashlight and mirror to view your eyes dilating. Turn the flashlight on, but point it down toward the ground away from your eyes. Try to look at your eyes in the mirror with very little light. The pupils should appear quite large. Continue looking in the mirror, but now bring the flashlight near your eyes. Don't shine it directly in your eyes. Watch your pupils contract rapidly.

WHAT'S GOING ON?

When night falls, a physical process begins in the human eye so that we can see better. The pupils begin to dilate or open up to let in any available light. Total dilation takes about 15 minutes.

When you get outside at night, you may not be able to see much at first. Stick around. Your eyes are undergoing a transformation, and pretty soon you'll have a good pair of night eyes! Try these easy activities, and read what's happening to your eyes.

disappearing act

Try this after you have been outside in the dark for at least 30 minutes. Stand about 10 feet away from a friend. Now, stare hard at each other's heads. Yikes, your friend's head has vanished! By the way, so has yours.

WHAT'S GOING ON?

The part of our eyes that processes light is called the *retina*. It contains many receptor cells called *rods* and *cones*. The rods help us to see in black and white. We have about 125 million rod cells.

Cones aid us in seeing color. We only have about 6½ million cone cells. Rods are mostly found around the outside or periphery of the retina, while the cones are found closer to the center of the retina.

When we're in darkness or low light situations, our rods slowly become saturated by a pigment called *rhodopsin* that helps us to see better. It takes about 45 minutes for the rhodopsin to totally saturate the rods and give us our best night vision.

We're accustomed to staring at objects that we're trying to see in low light environments. However, when we stare at something in the dark, we're

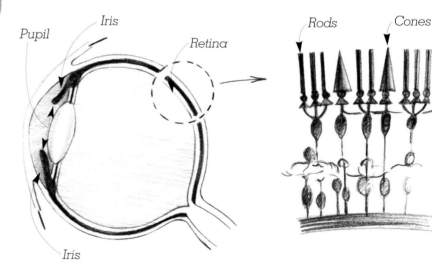

Illustrated side view of an eye

night animal vision

mostly using our cones in the center of the retina instead of our rods. The cones do not function very well in the dark, so it appears that the object disappears.

Nocturnal animals can see at night much better than we can. Why? They have many more rods than we do. If you happen to catch an animal with the glare of your flashlight one night, notice the reflection their eyes have from the shining light. This reflection is actually a layer of shiny material at the back of their eyes that helps the animal's eyes receive even more light because the light gets reflected back through the eye.

what is it?

Place one object far enough away that your partner can barely see it, but can't identify it. Instruct him to begin walking in the direction of the object. He should move his eyes back and forth rather than stare at the object. How close did he have to get to identify it? Now have him go back to the same starting point. Replace the object with a similar-looking object (so that he doesn't know what it is). Tell him to try walking toward it again, this time just staring at the object. Did he have to get closer to identify it?

WHAT'S GOING ON?

Since our rods are best suited to help us see at night, it is helpful to shift your eyes around to see better, rather than stare at something.

color confusion

Bring a bunch of markers outside with you. After being in the dark for at least 30 minutes, start randomly pulling markers out of the box, and, just using your "night vision," write the name of the color you think the marker is on a piece of paper. Do this with all the markers.

The next time you're inside, check to see how well you did. Boy, did your eyes mess up.

WHAT'S GOING ON?

The cones that help us see in color don't work well without light.

wolf howl

This activity isn't to attract wolves, but to simply chat with them a bit. You don't even have to leave the safety of your campfire or campsite.

WHAT YOU NEED

A bunch of friends
A location where there
    might be wolves

WHAT YOU DO

1 Stand facing what you decide is the deepest part of the wilderness.

2 Start with one person (your loudest friend) throwing her head back and giving a great big, long, deep howl.

3 Get really quiet, and listen for a reply. After a minute, try again.

4 If you're not getting a response, let everyone in on the fun. After 15 to 30 seconds, make everyone stop. Listen for a reply. If you do get a reply, stop howling, since the wolves won't answer you again for about an hour or so.

WHY WOLVES HOWL

To claim their territory

To call to other members of their pack

To celebrate the beginning or end of a hunt

Or, as you may have just found out, to have a little fun

look up!

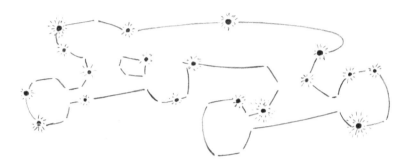

Many ancient civilizations created stories to try to explain the night sky. There are thousands of myths based on the patterns of stars called *constellations*. They gave them names and created stories to describe them. You can do the same.

WHAT YOU NEED

A starry night
A friend or two

WHAT YOU DO

1 Choose an open spot outside where there aren't a lot of trees and there isn't much light. This will give you the best view of the night sky.

2 Lie down on your back, and have your friends do the same so that your heads are nearly touching. Look up. Give your eyes at least 15 minutes to adjust to the darkness.

3 If you look to the side of a star instead of directly at it, you can see it better. Do some of the stars look like they're different colors? That's because they are made of different gases. Some stars appear red, others blue, and others white or yellowish.

a north american myth

4 Find a pattern of stars, and create your own picture. Maybe it's a horse or lion, a boat, a mountain, a picture of a person—the sky's the limit! Name your picture.

5 Now think of a story to go along with your picture, and take turns telling the stories you came up with. When you get back to a place with light, write down your story, and draw pictures of your very own constellations.

INCREDIBLE STARS

We can't touch them, smell them, or even begin to imagine how big they really are. No one in our lifetime or many lifetimes after ours will even get remotely close to one. In fact, light takes over four years to travel to us from the nearest star, *Proxima Centauri*. Some stars are already dead, and we're just now seeing their light because they're so far away.

A long time ago, the sun always shone—there was no night. At this time, the animals of earth fought constantly, and no one got along. The creator, angry at all the commotion, punished the creatures by pulling a blanket over the sky. Night fell, and it was dark all the time. The animals, so used to daylight, were now scared. They decided to work together, and try to find a solution.

First, the bears and deer climbed on top of each other to create a tall pyramid to reach the sky. But the bears were so heavy they fell to the earth.

Next, the animals persuaded the eagle to fly and reach the sky. But the eagle became so tired that he did not have enough energy to pull off the blanket.

Feeling defeated, the creatures were about to give up. Then, the little hummingbird spoke up: "I can fly to the top of the blanket; I know I can."

The rest of the animals agreed to let her try. The hummingbird flew as fast as she could up toward the blanket. She reached it, but since she was so small, she couldn't pull the blanket off. Instead, she poked tiny holes all over it with her long, sharp beak. Everywhere she left a hole, the light from the sun shone through.

The creator was so pleased with how the animals had solved their problem together that he decided to remove the blanket every 12 hours. But, to remind everyone to keep cooperating, the blanket with stars would cover the sky for the next 12 hours ... for eternity.

"what's lurking out there" bug sheet

Whatever you do, don't use your mom's good white sheets for this project. It may *really* bug her.

WHAT YOU NEED
Large white sheet
Clothespins
Rocks
Flashlight

WHAT YOU DO

1 Tie a rope to two trees or other objects. Make sure it's taut. (See "Knuts about Knots" on page 36.)

2 Place the sheet over the rope, setting up a sort of viewing screen. Use the clothespins to keep the sheet from blowing off the rope, and stretch the sheet to the ground, and place rocks to weigh it down.

3 At night, turn on the flashlight and direct its light onto the sheet. Wait for bugs.

4 Get as close as you can, and collect a few specimens to study before returning them to the wild. What did you come up with?

Moths and other insects are more than dumb bugs who keep cooking themselves on your front porch light. The bugs around lights at night are just a little confused, and who can blame them! Certain insects have learned how to use the moon to navigate. They keep the moon in a fixed location, allowing them to determine their line of movement. This worked just fine until about 100 years ago when street and porch lights started popping up around the world, and suddenly, the moon wasn't the brightest light around. As insects attempt to navigate using your porch light, which is much closer to them than the moon, they end up right at the light.

moth social club

This activity attracts moths three different ways. First: The moths are attracted to the light. Second: The moths stay to eat. Third: Female moths caught in the box attract male moths.

WHAT YOU NEED

1 teaspoon of warm orange juice
1 teaspoon of mashed overripe banana
2 tablespoons water
Small plate
Shoebox
Light source
Screen, cut at least 1-inch longer and wider than the opening of the box

WHAT YOU DO

1 Mix the orange juice, banana, and water on the plate, and carefully place the plate in the shoebox.

2 At night, turn on the flashlight or other source of light, and place the box under it. Wait for moths.

3 Once you have several moths feeding on the plate, place the screen over the box.

4 Without letting the moths go, try to take the plate out. Don't spill. Keep the light on.

5 If moths keep landing on the screen, even without food to attract them, then you've trapped some female moths who are giving off a *scent* called *pheromones*, which male moths can smell up to several miles away. When you're done, let the moths go.

FUN MOTH FACTS

Most moths are nocturnal.

Though moths are usually considered butterflies' ugly second cousin, moths, like the lunar moth, can be quite beautiful and amazing to observe.

There are approximately 20,000 species of butterflies in the world and over 100,000 different kinds of moths.

Many moths have awesome names. Here are just a few: hawk moth, death's head hawk moth, elephant hawk moth, garden tiger moth.

sound map

Since your eyes aren't going to see much at night, it's time to train your ears to explore the night and its many unusual sounds.

WHAT YOU NEED

An adult partner
Notebook
Pencil
Red plastic acetate or
   red cellophane
Flashlight

WHAT YOU DO

1 Choose a trail that you're familiar with during the day. That evening, hike it for a few minutes, then find a comfortable place to sit.

2 Put an "X" in the center of one page of your notebook. This symbolizes where you're sitting.

3 Sit as quietly as possible, back to back with your partner, and listen for at least 10 minutes. For every sound you hear, place a dot on the paper in the direction and distance that you think it came from. Try to identify each sound.

4 When you're finished, compare notes with your partner. How many of the same sounds did you hear? Did you identify any sounds as the same thing? What were some unusual sounds you heard?

MY EARS ARE BETTER THAN YOUR EARS!

So says many of those nocturnal animals you're trying to listen to. If you cup your hand behind your ears, you'll be able to hear a little bit better, but by no means anywhere as well as a hare or fox. Your ears are smaller, and you can't move them around like they can.

night animal

3 The second group hides in the woods just off the trail, but no more than 5 feet away from it.

4 The first group then proceeds along the trail to finish the hike. If the second group can remain hidden quietly until the first group walks by, they have succeeded! They are official night animals.

5 Switch groups and try it again!

Imagine you're a nocturnal animal that must remain quiet when your predator is around in order to survive. Could you do it?

WHAT YOU NEED
At least 4 people
  (the more the better)
Red-acetate-covered
  flashlight (optional)

WHAT YOU DO

1 Choose a trail that everyone knows well. Begin hiking together.

2 One group should stop and wait about 2 or 3 minutes (or count to 100), while the second group hikes ahead on the trail at least 50 yards. Make sure there are adults in both groups.

recording night sounds

Use a tape recorder and a microphone to capture the sounds of the great outdoors.

WHAT YOU NEED
Tape recorder
Audiotape
Microphone (optional)
Long stick (optional)
Rubber band or clamp
  (optional)

WHAT YOU DO

1 Pick your spot for recording the night sounds. Make sure it's not too close to any campsites or other "people noise." Take along an adult partner while looking for an appropriate place.

2 Place the recorder with the tape in it on a rock or other high-and-dry location; press record; and either sit there quietly, or attempt to get away without making too much noise. If you're going to sit there as you tape, listen to the tape as soon as you're done. Did you hear any sounds you didn't notice as you recorded? Our ears are good editors of sound.

3 You can also use a microphone and attach it to a long stick with a rubber band or clamp. Use the stick to get the microphone up close to nature noises either at night or during the day. You can capture the sounds of insects, birds, frogs, etc.

parabolic reflector

WHAT YOU DO

1 Tape triangular-shaped aluminum pieces to the inside of the umbrella.

2 Tape the microphone to the stem of the umbrella, facing into the umbrella about 5 inches from the aluminum-covered inside.

3 Do a few test runs, and see how well it's picking up sound. Move the microphone up and down the stem to figure out where the best spot is. Your reflector may be able to pick up noises more than a few hundred feet away.

This crazy-looking contraption is not the most convenient thing to carry around while exploring nature, but if you want your recorder to pick up more sound, then give it a try sometime. The umbrella acts as a sound-gathering dish.

WHAT YOU NEED
Umbrella
Aluminum foil
Duct tape
Microphone
Recorder
Audiotape

appendix

classifying all living things

All the millions of living things on this planet are divided into a series of groups and subgroups depending on how closely related they are.

First of all, all living things are divided into five kingdoms:
- Plants
- Fungi
- Animals
- Protoctista
- Bacteria

Then, animals are divided into *phyla* (singular *phylum*), and plants are divided into *divisions*. Living things in these groups have important characteristics in common, even if they may be quite different in some ways. For example, humans are in the same phylum as bullfrogs and guinea pigs.

Phyla (*divisions* for plants) are then divided into *classes*.

Classes are divided into *orders*.

Orders are divided into *families*.

Families are divided into *genera*.

Finally, animals are sorted into *species*. (Animals of the same species can reproduce).

This whole classification system is known as *taxonomy*. Sometimes these classifications are broken down into sub-classes.

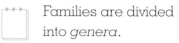

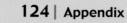

THE NAME GAME

Animals and plants have more than one name, and sometimes, to add to the confusion, they share names. To fix this problem, scientists use a two-part Latin name to label each species of animal. The first word is the organism's *genus*, and the second name is just for that one species.

Do you need to know any of this information to enjoy nature? No, but this is useful information if you like field guides, or if you want to learn something more about what you're exploring.

YOUR TAXONOMY

Kingdom: *Animal*
Phylum: *Chordata*
Class: *Mammalia*
Order: *Primata*
Family: *Hominidae*
Genus: *Homo*
Species: *Sapien*
Your Latin name: *Homo Sapien*

TAXONOMY OF YOUR DOG

Kingdom: *Animal*
Phylum: *Chordata*
Class: *Mammalia*
Order: *Carnivora*
Family: *Canidae*
Genus: *Canis*
Species: *Familiarus*
Dog's Latin name:
   Canis Familiarus

You and your dog (or cat) share the same kingdom, phylum, and class, but that's where the similarities end. Thank goodness.

metric conversion table

Inches	Centimeters	Inches	Centimeters
⅛	3 mm	12	30
¼	6 mm	13	32.5
⅜	9 mm	14	35
½	1.3	15	37.5
⅝	1.6	16	40
¾	1.9	17	42.5
⅞	2.2	18	45
1	2.5	19	47.5
1¼	3.1	20	50
1½	3.8	21	52.5
1¾	4.4	22	55
2	5	23	57.5
2½	6.25	24	60
3	7.5	25	62.5
3½	8.8	26	65
4	10	27	67.5
4½	11.3	28	70
5	12.5	29	72.5
5½	13.8	30	75
6	15	31	77.5
7	17.5	32	80
8	20	33	82.5
9	22.5	34	85
10	25	35	87.5
11	27.5	36	90

index

PHOTO CREDITS

Key: l = left; r = right; t=top;
c=center; b=bottom

John Widman: cover, pages 36 (l) and 118
Sandra Stambaugh: cover: leaf/berry and red maple
Dave Maslowski: pages 8 (bl), 32 (bl), 62, 54 (r), 64, 113 (r)
Seattle Support Group: cover: red beetle
Corbis: cover: raccoon
Photodisc: page 26 (tl)
Getty Images: pages 3, 5, 6, 7, 8 (tr, c), 9 (c), 10 (r), 15 (b), 24, 25 (tl), 28 (br), 66 (r), 75 (b), 82 (l), 84 (r), 85 (r), 86, 87, 88 (b), 89 (b), 90 (t), 93 (tl), 94 (r), 95 (t), 97 (tr), 102 (bl); 104 (tr); 105 (r); 105 (b); 122 (tr)
Brand X Pictures: 35 (tr), 67 (l), 72 (bl), 73 (bc), 77 (c) and (tr), 78 (br); 119 (r); and 120 (tc)
Stock Photography Online: page 100 (b)
National Oceanic and Atmospheric

Administration/Department of Commerce: pages 12 (tl), 98 (bl), 99 (tl), 103 (tl) by Richard B. Mieremet, 104 (bl) by Frank Ruopoli
USDA Agricultural Research Services: page 23 (bl),
NASA: page 117
U. S. Fish and Wildlife Service: pages 23 (r); 38 (tl), photo by Steve Chase; 42 (b l); 43 (tl); 47 (tl), photo by John and Karen Hollingsworth; 47 (tr), photo by John and Karen Hollingsworth; 47 (bl), photo by Kate Banish; 49; 51[c], photo by Lynn Llewellyn; 51(b), photo by Carl Burger; 51 (tr); 52 (l), photo by John and Karen Hollingsworth; 54 (r); 58; 61; 63 (l), photo by Dave Menke; 65, photo by S. Maslowski; 66 (tr), photo by James C. Leupold; 75 (t), photo by Ed Loth; 100 (tl), photo by Hans Stuart; 109, photo by Richard A. Coon; 111 (l), photo by John and Karen Hollingsworth; 115 (r), photo by Tracy Brooks; 120 (tr); 121 (br), photo by LuRay Parker; 124 (l), photo by Denny Bingham; and 124 (r)
US Army Corps of Engineers: 40, 43 (br), 66 (bl), 66 (br), 79 (tl), 98 (tl), and 103 (br)